HEART, SOUL, MIGHT

MEDITATIONS ON KNOWING AND LOVING GOD

by the faculty of
Central Baptist Theological Seminary of Minneapolis

KEVIN T. BAUDER

EDITOR

CENTRAL SEMINARY PRESS
Minneapolis, Minnesota

Published by:
Central Seminary Press
900 Forestview Lane North
Plymouth, Minnesota 55441
(phone) 763.417.8250
(fax) 763.417.8258
www.centralseminary.edu
info@centralseminary.edu

Printed by:
Nystrom Publishing Company, Inc.
9100 Cottonwood Lane North
Maple Grove, Minnesota 55369

ISBN: 978-0-9838766-0-1
LCCN: 2011936484

Printed in the United States of America.

Unless otherwise indicated, all Scripture quotations are from
the King James Version.

CONTENTS

i

Foreword

$\mathcal{T}$he book you are reading is the product of the faculty at Central Baptist Theological Seminary of Minneapolis. It is a collection of poems, prayers, and essays in devotional theology or, if you prefer, theological devotion. We judged these chapters to be necessary because we believe that devotion and theology should never be separated. As we see it, our devotion is inescapably informed by our theology, and our theology fails in its purpose unless it terminates in devotion. This is what it means to love God with all our heart, soul, and might.

All of the selections in this book combine devotion with theology, but the balance varies from piece to piece. Some are more theological, while others are more devotional. In general, the prayers and poems are more devotional, while some of the essays are more theological.

In planning the volume, each professor was allowed to decide what he wanted to write. No restrictions were placed on topics—indeed, our sense is that every aspect of Christian practice and doctrine will ultimately point to those perfections of the divine nature that lead us to devotion. Professors were also allowed their choice of literary genres. Once the selections were in hand, I arranged them more-or-less by topic.

The professors of Central Seminary are united in important areas of the faith. They are all Baptists, dispensationalists, cessationists, and separatists. They all reject that form of revivalism that bases Christian progress mainly upon a succession of crisis decisions. Outside of these areas, however, they exhibit significant diversity. They take varying positions on issues over which Christians often disagree. This book makes no effort to downplay their diversity. We enjoy our differences and the conversations that they engender. Not every theological position taken by every professor in this book should be attributed to the faculty as a whole.

This volume could not have been published without the labors of many individuals. Three in particular deserve the authors' thanks. Deborah Forteza, former director of publications at Central Seminary, prepared the work for publication. Debra Bauder provided a skilled set of eyes for proofreading. Grant Bird standardized the Scriptural citations in the volume. These three have eliminated many problems from the rough manuscript, but (of course) they bear no responsibility for any errors that remain.

In their citation of Scripture, the authors used a variety of versions in their original essays. This diversity was undesirable for a number of reasons, and so the decision was made to employ the King James Version in all quotations of the biblical text. The only exception to this rule occurs where authors have given their own translations from the original languages.

These essays are sent forth with the prayer that they will enrich the lives of God's people. May they help you to know God better. May they help you to love Him more.

Kevin T. Bauder
Plymouth, Minnesota
September 2011

ONE

The Written Word of God

RATIONALISM AND MYSTICISM

Kevin T. Bauder

C hristian theology moves between two poles. On the one hand, it is impelled by the desire to understand God. Understanding implies explanation, and explanation is essentially a matter of giving reasons. This impulse leads us to ask why God is thus or does so. If we cannot find clear reasons, then we at least seek for careful definitions. We may not be able to say *why* God is Triune, but we at least attempt to formulate as precisely as we can what the Trinity means. This theological pole could be called the *rational* impulse in theology.

At the other pole, theologians constantly bump up against the recognition that God is transcendent. They quickly learn that the predicates that we apply to God cannot be used univocally. Even so basic an assertion as "God exists" has to mean something different from the assertion that "we exist," for God's being is underived. He alone is self-existent—His being is different from our being.

Faced with the limitations of human understanding and human language, theologians sometimes despair of any rational knowledge of God. For them, theology becomes purely a matter of negation. They cannot meaningfully say what God is. They can only say what He is not. Rational knowledge of God is impossible.

In the place of rational knowledge, these theologians insert personal knowledge. On their understanding, God can be known directly and personally through His communion with the soul. What the soul learns of God in this encounter can never be verbalized, but it is real knowledge. This pole represents the *mystical* impulse in theology.

Both mysticism and rationalism can move into dangerous territory. Unbridled rationalism may sever itself from the text of Scripture, defining God's person and works according to speculative philosophical categories. In its eagerness to explain *why* God is this or does that, it may actually produce a kind of divine determinism in which the very freedom of God is denied. After all, a comprehensive explanation of why God does a thing is only a small step removed from an assertion that God had to do that thing. Ultimately, the rationalist conceives of God less as a person than as an abstract principle.

Other rationalists, eager to defend God's freedom, end up denying His nature. If God is bound by His nature (they reason), then He does not make truly free choices. Ockham argued that Christ could have become incarnate as something other than a human being. That He chose to become a man was His voluntary choice, or else He was not free when He made it.

Like rationalism, mysticism may also sever itself from the biblical text. If the true knowledge of God is ineffable and indefinable, then Scripture serves only as a sort of on-ramp to the highway of mystical experience. It is not itself a revelation of God. The Bible is ultimately unnecessary.

The problem for mysticism is that purely negative theology ends up contradicting itself. Theologians who say that they cannot know anything about God are actually asserting that they do know at least one thing about God, namely, His unknowability. If these theologians are right, then they necessarily have to be wrong.

The alternative to both pure rationalism and pure mysticism is biblicism. Biblicists may be rational in that they intend to define and explain God's character and deeds. They may also be mystical insofar as they seek personal communion with God.

Biblicists, however, begin with Scripture. They see in biblical revelation the sole and sufficient source of authority for their knowledge of God.

Biblicists do exercise their rational capacities. They discover much reasoning within the text of Scripture itself. Furthermore, they seek to draw sound inferences from explicitly biblical teachings. For biblicists, the mind is in full play.

Biblicists also respond to the mystical impulse, for at their best they desire personal communion with God. This communion, however, is enabled by and mediated through the text of Scripture. The God with whom they commune is not one whom they find by examining their own souls. He is one who lives and breathes within the pages of Holy Writ.

Left to themselves, both rationalism and mysticism push toward dangerous extremes. While each points up the problem with the other, they cannot be used to balance each other out. Only a proper biblicism can do that.

For a committed Biblicist, both the rational and the mystical impulse can be satisfied. The genuine biblicist will place both the mind and the heart in play all the time. Biblicists can give full rein to the desire to define and explain, while at the same time giving full rein to the yearning to know God personally. Only within Biblicism do these two impulses achieve full harmony.

Biblicists rightly recoil from the extremes to which rationalism and mysticism can lead. Fear of the extremes may tempt them to stifle the mind, the heart, or both. If they are genuine biblicists, however, this fear is unwarranted. Biblicism itself is what keeps both reason and mystical communion within their proper spheres. Loyalty to Scripture will restrain, discipline, and inform both impulses.

ON READING THE BIBLE

Kevin T. Bauder

*I*f the Bible is God's Word, then why does it come to us as such an (apparently) random collection of diverse literature? In one place we find stories, in another, legal codes, and in another, epic poetry. Here we read correspondence and there we discover verses of song. Some documents contain didactic reasoning while others give us apocalypses.

Would it not have been better if God had simply sent us an inspired and inerrant systematic theology? Or better still, He might have given us two lists: one of propositions to believe about Himself and the other of commands for us to obey. Would not life and faith be simpler?

Nevertheless, we have been given the Bible. God is the one who gave it. God is the one who inspired it. God is the one who commands its use. Why is the Bible that we have better than a systematic theology (however perfect) or a list of propositions and obligations?

The fundamental reason is that no list of propositions can possibly communicate the multi-faceted glory of God. God is infinite in His majesty and, consequently, infinitely variegated in His splendor. Part of the purpose of the Bible is to help us glimpse the many dimensions of God's grandeur.

That would be difficult—perhaps impossible—to do with mere theological propositions. True, God could give us a proposition to the effect that His glory has many dimensions. We could read such a proposition and intellectually affirm it without ever beginning to glimpse the glory itself. God does not simply want us to know and affirm that He is glorious, however. He wishes us to behold His glory. He wishes to place Himself on display.

More than that, God wants us to *know* Him, and knowing Him is not at all the same thing as knowing *about* Him. We can learn about Him from propositions. We can gather theological data, categorize it, and discourse learnedly concerning the divine nature. This mass of data, however, will do us no good unless we know Him.

An analogy may clarify the difference. Consider a young man who notices a young woman and wants to get to know her. Through various machinations he secures copies of her medical records, her high school and college transcripts, and her bank statements. He hires a detective to investigate her, find out who her friends are, where she spends her time, and what her preferences are. He immerses himself in the reports and gains significant factual knowledge about her.

When the young woman finds out what he has been doing, she will not feel flattered. She is more likely to feel violated, and she would have every right to say, "Depart from me, I never knew you." She may speak to the police or seek an injunction from a court. Although the young man has mastered a great many facts, he does not know her. He has never developed a relationship with her. In the absence of a trusting relationship, his knowledge about her is an intrusion into her privacy and a violation of her personhood. The sooner his stalking ends, the better.

In our understanding of God, we often behave just like that young man. We treat the Bible the same way that the young man was treating the medical records, transcripts, and bank statements. We seek for factual data about God, but we do it in the absence of a personal, loving, and trusting relationship. We should not be surprised when God resists us and hides His face from us.

Reading the Bible ought to be like entering into a conversation. What we read should not terminate in our minds, but should pass on into our hearts. In turn, our hearts should respond to God's self-disclosure, welcoming it, treasuring it, reflecting upon it, and answering it. Our hearts should answer with adoration when God puts Himself on display. They should respond with obedience to His merest wish (let alone His command). They should respond with confession, with submission, with petition. Above all, they should respond with delight and rejoicing at having been invited into the innermost chamber of divine intimacy.

Too often, we draw a distinction between reading the Bible for study and reading the Bible for devotion. We read it for exegetical purposes, then we throw the switch and read it for edification. Another flip of the switch and we are studying for sermon preparation, but then we switch again and find ourselves in meditation mode.

This switching back and forth produces two problems. The first is a propensity to read the Bible academically without reading it devotionally. The toughest exegetical work should nevertheless yield fruit in our walk with God. The second problem is that if we keep flipping that switch, sooner or later it will get stuck, and it usually gets stuck in intellectual mode. When we accustom ourselves to reading the Bible for information only, we soon lose sight of the God whose communion we ought to crave.

The Bible does contain factual information about God, but that information is nearly always couched in the elements of personal encounter. We do not find factual abstractions in the pages of Scripture. Rather, we read stories about how God has worked in the lives of His people. We discover poems that express the innermost movements of spiritual experience. We meet vivid imagery that sparks our imaginations and draws us into God's work in the world. Indeed, the Bible taken as a whole is one long story—the story of God. As we read the story and enter into it, we do not simply encounter information. We encounter Him.

God makes Himself present in the pages of Scripture. The Bible is alive with His person and work. In the biblical tapestry of literary genres and authorial styles we find that God displays the manifold nature of His glory. He invites us into its pages in order that we might meet Him, know Him, and love Him. Because God is present in the Bible, it is our chief treasure on earth. If we have a Bible to read and nothing else, we are still inestimably rich. Let us not neglect the wealth that God has showered upon us.

THE TREASURED WORD

Roy Beacham

Oh how I love your law!
It is my meditation all the day.
Ps 119:97

Oh God, who far surpassing mortal thought or speech,
Still deigned through human scribe your searchless self to show
In smallest measure; fit for man to stretch and reach,
Yet vast enough through lifetime's work a morsel know.
Your word is all I own to tell me who you are,
The record penned, a footprint of your deity;
Nothing on earth could yet approach its value, far
Past unscaled heights, or endless depths of chartless sea.
Spur my desire to search this work you've finely wrought,
Frame my poor mind to comprehend its treasured fill,
Mold all my heart to love the truths you've kindly taught,
Grant me the faith to do your good and perfect will.

Two

The Purpose of God

THE GOD WHO CREATES AND BLESSES

Kevin T. Bauder

*W*e often assume that the opening chapters of Genesis are included in the Bible to satisfy our curiosity about origins. "Where did I come from?" is, after all, a perennial question. These chapters, however, do not seem to provide a compact answer to that question. They contain too much that is not relevant to it. Besides, how often does God reveal something in the Bible simply in order to satisfy our curiosity?

"Where did I come from?" is part of a bigger question, "Who am I?" which in turn leads to the questions "Why do I exist?" and "What does it all mean?" These questions together are not only perennial, they are fundamental to our humanity. And the Bible answers all of them by defining our identity in relation to God.

The creation narratives serve as the introduction to the literary corpus that we know as the Pentateuch, or the five books of Moses. These five books constitute a single narrative, a comprehensive literary whole. The entire narrative is focused upon the events that occur at Sinai, especially upon the giving of the Law. Therefore, a primary concern of the Pentateuch is the character of the God who reveals the Law.

God's Law is often viewed primarily as restrictive and punitive. It bars people from the illicit fulfillment of certain intense desires and it pronounces judgment upon those who pursue those illicit fulfillments. Sinful people naturally view the God of the Law as an angry and vengeful being. H. L. Mencken once quipped that Puritanism is the haunting fear that someone, somewhere, might be happy. Many—perhaps most—people perceive the God of Sinai just that way.

The opening chapters of Genesis completely subvert this false perception. From the very beginning, God is depicted as one who creates what is good. Seven times the opening chapter of Genesis has God declaring that creation is good, concluding with the observation that all that He made is "very good."

The term "good" is sometimes used of moral uprightness. Other times it is used of beneficence or usefulness. In Genesis 1 it almost certainly has the latter idea: things like light, trees, birds, and fish are useful. This leads to a question—for whom are such things useful?

The answer to that question also clarifies the focus of the creation narratives. The things God makes are useful for human beings. Those things are good because they are good for humanity. Consequently, the apex of the chapter is the creation of humanity. Humans are designed to enjoy the good things that God has made and (more importantly) to enjoy the Creator who made them.

The notion of goodness and enjoyment is reinforced in three ways. The first is the introduction of the blessing. After God created humanity as male and female, He blessed them with the capability to be fruitful and multiply, to exercise dominion, and to subdue the earth. The passage is often read as a mandate, but several reasons exist for taking it as a blessing. First, the language of blessing and the language of command are grammatically identical, so the grammar of this passage could be taken either way. Second, the text bluntly declares that this is a blessing, but it does not call it a mandate. Third, part of the language is virtually identical to the words God used in blessing the fish and birds earlier in the chapter, and no responsible interpreter would insist that God is giving a mandate to brute beasts. Fruitfulness, multiplication, dominion, and the subduing of the earth are not a task list but a blessing from God to humans.

The notion of goodness and enjoyment is also reinforced by the Sabbath rest. At the end of the creation week God rested on the seventh day, blessing and sanctifying that day. The connection of God's blessing and sanctification with rest on the seventh day seems to imply that this rest is one of the good things in God's creation. Humans are created in God's image. Therefore, if God rests, then they, too, should rest. The problem lies in trying to understand what "rest" means.

Clearly it cannot be taken to mean that God was tired and needed to "rest up." God does not get tired. He did not need to recuperate after a hard week of creation. Some other kind of rest must be in view.

An analogy may be helpful. Think of a man who spends a morning mowing the lawn, trimming the hedges, edging the walks, and weeding the flower beds. He is far from exhausted when he finishes, but he goes and pours himself a lemonade, plants a chair in the middle of the lawn, and sits down to rest. What is he doing? In what does his rest consist? Not merely in the relief of tired arms and legs, but in the opportunity to delight in the result of his labors. The new-mown lawn, the crisp edging, the orderly hedges: all of these are a pleasure to his eye, and he takes pleasure in them. He may briefly entertain the thought, "Hey—I'm really good."

This helps us to understand the quality of God's "rest" on the seventh day. He made nothing new. Rather, He surveyed what He had done and delighted Himself in it. At that point He might justly and without a bit of conceit have entertained the thought that He was indeed a marvelous creator.

By delighting Himself in His works and occupying Himself with His glory, He was setting a pattern for us. For us, "Sabbath rest" (whether it occurs on the seventh day or at some other time) means more than simple relief from weekly labors. It means pondering God's person, His mighty works, His blessings and gifts. It means recognizing His goodness and glory in all He has done. It means delighting ourselves in Him and in His good gifts—gifts that might include family, leisure, food and drink, or natural beauty, among others.

Finally, the notion of goodness and enjoyment is reinforced by the fact that God created humanity in His own image and likeness. Of course, theologians debate what that means. At minimum, it appears to imply that humanity is made for companionship with God. God wishes us to enjoy Him and to experience His goodness. That is why He made us.

The God who gave us a good creation is also the God of Sinai. The God who pronounced blessing upon us is also the God who gave the Law. From the first chapter of the first book of the Bible, God is depicted as infinitely benevolent. Such a God is worthy of our trust and obedience.

The goodness of this God is further highlighted in the second creation narrative (Gen 2:5-24). In this narrative, Moses recapitulates the story of creation with a significant shift in perspective. This retelling of the story allows him to focus our attention more specifically upon God's purpose for humanity.

Moses emphasizes God's goodness from the beginning of the account. The original creation had no weeds, no harsh weather, and no hard labor. Rather, God provided everything for the man whom He created, placing him in a garden or sheltered park. Moses specifies the location of this garden by naming four rivers that would have been familiar to the people of his day.

The Tigris (Hiddekel) and Euphrates are known to moderns. The Pison is unknown. The Gihon, while not known, is said to flow through the land of Cush. It may be another name for the Nile. It could also be another reference to the "River of Egypt" that evidently marked the border of that country.

In any case, Moses depicts Eden as a place that was larger than a farm or even a city. It stretched from modern-day Iraq all the way (approximately) to modern-day Egypt. The garden was larger than many entire nations. Incidentally, it also appears to correspond to the boundaries of the land that was later promised to Abraham (Gen 15:18), as well as the territory that was tributary to Solomon (2 Chr 9:26).

Eden was a beautiful park that God prepared for humanity. God "rested" the man in the Garden (Gen 2:15), which carries implications of shelter and safety. God caused trees to grow there for the man's nourishment. He also caused other trees to grow: the Tree of Life and the Tree of the Knowledge of Good and Bad.

The name of the second tree is what ties the two creation narratives together. The emphasis of the first account was on the goodness of the Creator. The second account re-emphasizes the Creator's benevolence in many ways. The expansive dimensions of the garden, its nature as a sheltered park, the provision of food, and above all God's provision of safety are factors that reflect the kind nature of the good God who blesses.

The tree also draws attention to God's purpose for humanity. The man is given a command to obey. Obedience should have been easy with an infinitely benevolent deity, and both creation narratives emphasize God's goodness repeatedly. This alerts readers that God is worth obeying, that His commands stem only from His interest in blessing humans.

That is why God confronts the man with the Tree of the Knowledge of Good and Bad. Throughout this context, *good* means *useful* or *beneficial*. This hints at the purpose of the tree. Surely it was a real tree with real fruit, but it was also a symbolic tree that represented the knowledge of good and bad.

To this point in the narrative, God has always been the one to say what is good. Human responsibility has consisted entirely in the willingness to receive whatever good the Creator has provided. Human knowledge of the bad is non-existent, and human knowledge of the good is a derived knowledge that comes strictly from trusting the Creator. Therefore, the tree must represent the intention for the man to determine good and bad for himself. If the man will not trust the Creator to determine what is good, then he will have to decide for himself. He will gain his own knowledge of good and bad.

In other words, what was being tested was Adam's willingness to trust God. By refusing to eat of the tree, the man would be submitting himself to God's decisions about what was good and what was bad. If he ate the fruit of the tree, however, his eating would constitute his declaration of independence from God and his choice to determine good and bad for himself. This apparently insignificant act would really constitute the worst sort of treason, for it would imply that the man now considered the Creator to be untrustworthy. In this test, obedience and trust are inextricably linked.

If the man rejected the Creator, pronounced Him untrustworthy, and declared independence, he would come under sentence of death. How could it be otherwise? The Creator is the origin of life. To separate one's self from Him is to choose death. God warned that if the man ate the fruit of the Tree of the Knowledge of Good and Bad, then the sentence of death would be passed on the same day.

At this point, all of the pieces are in place for the great drama of temptation that will follow in Genesis 3. Before the man is allowed to face temptation, however, one further episode intervenes. This episode begins when God declares that something is *not* good. He says that it is not good for the man to be alone, and He purposes to make for the man a helper "like himself." This comes to the reader as a surprise, because up until this point everything has been *very* good. Why choose this stage of the narrative at which to announce what is not good?

The crucial question is whether the Creator really deserves the trust that He requires from the man. Can humans truly rely upon the Creator to supply everything that is good for them? Will the Creator notice any deficiencies, and can He be trusted to supply them?

God was aware of Adam's need even before Adam detected it. In fact, God had to show Adam the need by putting him through an exercise in taxonomy. By comparing and classifying (naming) animals, the man discovered that he was alone in the world. No one else like him existed.

God was now in the position to meet the need. He caused a deep sleep to fall upon Adam, took one of his ribs, and fashioned a woman. He then brought her to the man and presented her to him. Adam's response takes the form of the first poem to be composed by any human being.

> She is bone of my bones,
> Flesh of my flesh,
> She shall be called *Ishah*,
> Because she was taken out of *Ish*.

Adam's poem draws attention to the likeness between the man and the woman, which in turn provides the basis for the intimacy that God intended them to enjoy. This is an expression of ecstatic joy. Not only did the Creator notice the need before Adam was even aware of it, but He also met the need in a way that was beyond anything Adam could imagine.

The Creator God—our God—is absolutely worthy of our trust. He is good and benevolent by His very nature. He desires our trust and obedience, but He does not compel it. To worship God by our trust and obedience is the thing for which we were made. It is our highest good, and no lesser good can ever satisfy us.

ΕΥΧΑΡΙΣΤΩΜΕΝ
LET US GIVE THANKS

Kevin T. Bauder

O Father of lights, with Whom is neither variableness nor shadow of turning, from Your hand receive we every gift, each one good and perfect. Naught have we of our own; nothing do we possess that we were not given. Our open hands know not for what they grasp, but discover themselves filled with goodness and blessing from Your bounty.

You are life. You have life in Yourself. You are the source of all living. Our being, frail and small, races ever toward dissolution. Our little existences, propped up moment by moment from without, depend incessantly upon You. Ceaselessly Your life-gift pours into us, else we would straight away unform, undo, and unbe. Without life from Your Life, we could neither stand, nor sense, nor say, nor even sin. Your Life is the light that ignites our own tiny sparks.

Made like beasts as to our bodies, we share their need for breath. Athirst, we cannot even weep without water. Hungered, we cannot endure without food. Naked, we cannot abide without cover. Weary, we cannot mend without rest. Your eye, which sees the sparrow's plight, perceives our want. Your bounty, which clothes the lilies, attends to our lack. From Your good hand receive we bread and breath, hearth and health.

Made within like You (splendid likeness!) we stand on display, images of Your self-disclosure, each a little lens to focus Your perfections in the eyes of our fellows. Like Your own dance, step-to-three, in eternal, transparent, intertwining compenetration, so do our meetings and partings, our greetings and doings, signify Your personhood. Not made for ourselves, we crave other eyes to peer through us into Your selfless self. Thus we yearn for love and trust and human care, for we are Your image. Before we know our need, You, who hold counsel from eternity, have already encircled us with multiplied intimacies. Or ever we can speak their names, You grant us parents, brothers, and friends. Before we grasp their purpose, You bestow spouses and children. Delights these are indeed, but not private enjoyments. Lacking their eyes to focus upon You, our little lens would grow dark and our purpose remain empty. Our fulfillment lies in making You seen, in magnifying Your perfections for the eyes of others. We need Him whom we image; we need also them to whom we image. Your infinite wisdom has foreseen and fore-granted our need in goodness and mercy.

Mirrors we are, made to reflect your person, but mirrors now shattered. Eager to see ourselves in ourselves, we did twist back upon ourselves and did burst the glass. We cannot paste ourselves back into place, for the broken facets of our visage now reflect a contorted mosaic. Is brokenness better than unbeing? Yet still we bend, and twist, and burst again the shards.

You might have swept us aside. In what desolate place should we lie, forever contemned, cast out as a danger? What need have You of shattered glass?

But we are not rejected! For He, in whose likeness we are, came finally to be in our likeness, too. The Original (without ceasing to be original) became image; the Countenance (without ceasing to be the countenance) became mirror. Into our brokenness this Firstborn mediates and radiates the one, flawless representation of Your invisible perfection. Made one of us, but unbroken, He shines as You meant us to shine, and more! For He is we unbroken, and He is You.

Into the vast, liquid expanse of Your brightness You gather all the broken bits of our shattered visage. To be forgiven is not to be ignored! For the sake of His infinite pain You take infinite pains with every still-reflecting splinter. What we could never repair, He refashions in Himself, and out of brokenness You create variegated vessels of glory, reflecting and refracting perfection in thousand-fold splendor.

Thus You are making us in Him. From You we receive the forgiveness of sins (so freely! so freely!), not so that we may escape the pains of brokenness, but so that Your countenance may be seen in its utter wholeness. When the glory of Your presence finally bursts upon every eye, our once-shattered fragments, now redeemed and fused and shaped by Your grace, will sparkle and glisten with the manifold perfection of Your being. Finite eyes that could never comprehend the Whole will behold in our multiplied facets each reflected aspect of Your goodness and greatness and glory.

O Lord Who fills all in all, we marvel at Your great gifts: life and breath, provision and relation, redemption and glorification. These gifts are not many, but one. You have made us for Yourself, to be Your possession, but You have given Yourself to us as our lot and portion. We rejoice, for in the end nothing satisfies us except You, and nothing fulfills us except to be Yours. This is the delight of our souls: to gaze upon You, to behold Your perfection, to lose ourselves so completely in You that we become more truly ourselves than we have ever been, and to know that You are God.

For Yours is the Kingdom, and the power, and the glory forever. Amen.

THE GRANDEUR OF ELECTION

Jonathan Pratt

*B*efore "Michael Jordan" became the standard answer to the question, "Who is the greatest basketball player ever?" another high-leaping player caught my attention. Known as "Dr. J," his name was Julius Erving. He could make amazing leaps and gravity-defying dunks.

Back in those days I often dreamed of growing to be able to leap with similar alacrity, astounding the fans with my incredible dunking ability. I am still dreaming. Sadly, for people like me (name one Swede who can dunk a basketball) this feat will always be an impossibility.

Spiritual limitations can likewise affect people's hopes and dreams. Most people hope to go to heaven, but they face an undeniable spiritual problem. Theologians refer to this problem as depravity. Just like the man whose physical capacities eliminate the possibility of dunking, depravity eliminates the moral ability to believe in Jesus for salvation (Rom 3:11; Eph 2:1-3; Col 2:13a). But thankfully God makes the spiritually unattainable to be possible. In His great love and mercy God chooses to enable spiritually dead people to believe.

Many verses speak of God's choosing unbelievers to salvation: Ephesians 1:4 (According as he hath chosen us in him before the foundation of the world); Ephesians 1:11 (In whom also we have obtained an inheritance, being predestinated according to the purpose of him who worketh all things after the counsel of his own will); 2 Thessalonians 2:13 (God hath from the beginning chosen you to salvation); Acts 13:48 (as many as were ordained [chosen] to eternal life believed). In several cases believers are referred to as God's elect or chosen ones (Rom 11:7; Col 3:12; 1 Thess 1:4; 1 Pet 1:1; 2:9).

If God does the choosing, however, does not this create a major problem for us? What about the people who are not elected? Is God not unfair to choose some but not others? Inevitably, questions like these come to mind whenever we talk about the doctrine of election.

Perhaps the problems that arise in our minds with regard to election are due more to our inadequate understanding of the Bible's instruction about this doctrine than they are to God's so-called lack of fairness and compassion. Of course, there are those who try to help God out at this point by arguing against *total* depravity and by basing God's election on His foreknowledge of human willingness to believe. But solutions like these fail to find support in the biblical data.[1]

I would like to walk through the biblical data about God's election and then answer some of the common objections offered in opposition to this doctrine. The Bible reveals that God has *purposes* for election, *people* He elects, and a *time* when He elects.

The first issue involves God's purpose for election. Far from choosing humans based on their merit, God elected His children because of His own purpose and grace (2 Tim 1:9). Paul reveals this purpose of God in election while answering objections raised by those who cannot understand it. In Romans 9:22-23 the Bible asks, "What if God, willing *to shew his wrath*, and *to make his power known*, endured with much longsuffering the vessels of wrath fitted to destruction: And *that he might make known the*

---

[1]Some have suggested that the effects of humanity's depravity or inability are counteracted by God's "prevenient grace." This grace makes everyone capable of believing in Christ for salvation. See Millard Erickson, *Christian Theology*, vol. 3 (Grand Rapids: Baker, 1985), 919-920, 925, for a helpful description and refutation of this concept.

riches of his glory on the vessels of mercy, which he had afore prepared unto glory?" I have italicized the three main purposes behind God's election: to demonstrate His wrath, His power, and His glory.

Some might object to this type of display. We might be led to believe that a display of God's mercy and grace would suffice to adequately demonstrate the glory of God. Why the need for wrath and power as well? The short answer is that God is not just merciful and gracious; He is also holy and just. God is not afraid to reveal the many contours of Himself to us. In fact, Donald Westblade argues that if God "feels constrained to hide some aspect of his glory, he falsely implies that something about him is shameful." Westblade continues, "If [God] does not magnify the full extent of his glory, he fails to be completely loving to those for whom his glory is their highest delight, for he withholds from them something of himself that is grand." [2] Since God has, as the primary purpose of His election, a desire to magnify His glory to His children, we ought to put our hands over our mouths (Job 40:4) and bow in worship.

The second issue involves the people whom God elected. Did God choose particular individuals, or did He choose a generic group of people when He made the decree to elect "before the foundation of the world" (Eph 1:4)? If God did choose individuals, then was His choice based on His foreknowledge of their faith in Him or was election based upon His own predestinating will? I will address these questions in reverse order.

Some argue that verses like 1 Peter 1:2 (elect according to the foreknowledge of God) prove that God's reason for

---

[2]Donald J. Westblade, "Divine Election in the Pauline Literature," in *Still Sovereign*, ed. Thomas Schreiner and Bruce Ware (Grand Rapids: Baker, 2000), 86.

choosing certain people is based on His foreseeing their positive response to the gospel. There are three major problems with this understanding of God's foreknowledge. First, it suggests that the ultimate determining factor in one's salvation is personal ability to respond in faith to the gospel, but this view does not accord with Scripture's teaching about human depravity. Second, 2 Timothy 1:9 states that God has "called us with an holy calling, not according to our works, but according to his own purpose and grace." Clearly God's calling of us to salvation has nothing to do with any good act, even the act of believing. Third, numerous passages suggest that *foreknowledge* means much more than simply knowing ahead of time. The word is often used in connection with predestination (Acts 2:23; Rom 8:29) and several verses show that foreknowledge entails God's eternal personal electing commitment to those He knows (Rom 11:1-2; 1 Pet 1:20; Gal 4:9).

Several interpreters have sought to bypass their discomfort with election by arguing that God chose a group or category of people rather than particular individuals for salvation. This argument is generally based on the fact that Romans 9 speaks of the election of Israel (a group) rather than particular individuals. But a careful reading of Romans 9-11 indicates that both corporate and individual application should be made in regard to election. Paul includes several references to individuals using singular pronouns (9:15-21), and he includes an individual (himself) among the believing remnant (a group) in 11:1. The pursuit of righteousness by works as described in 9:30-10:21 cannot be taken corporately since clearly some individuals among Israel are saved by grace, even though Paul's language appears to include all of Israel. Apart from these passages in Romans 9-11, several other passages indicate that God elects particular individuals to salvation (Eph 1:4; 2 Thess 2:13; 2 Tim 1:9).

Apparently, Scripture teaches that God elected particular individuals. Consequently, election is *personal*. Election is also *unconditional* in that it is based upon God's sovereign decision before the creation of the world and not upon His foreseeing of the good merits of anyone.

The third issue has to do with the time of God's election. The Bible removes all question about this by declaring that it occurred before the creation of the world (Eph 1:4). This concept is further substantiated by the terms "predestination" or "foreordination" (Rom 8:29-30; Eph 1:5, 11) and "foreknowledge" (Rom 8:29; 1 Pet 1:2). There are several significant ramifications related to this timing of God's election. It is *efficacious* or certain, and it is unchanging or *immutable*. Though we do not know whom God has elected, we do know that He has already determined who will be saved. For this reason we must continue to strive for the salvation of lost souls in our witness, and we ought to give thanks to God for the privilege of being included in His eternal plan of redemption.

THE JUSTICE AND MERCY OF ELECTION

Jonathan Pratt

*A*s the pleasant aroma of freshly brewed coffee wafts across the room every morning in my home, the only satisfaction that I gain is olfactory. To me, coffee fails the two essential tests of an acceptable beverage: temperature (too hot) and taste (too bitter). My wife, on the other hand, thoroughly enjoys her daily cup, having acquired the necessary taste for this (to her way of thinking) simple, God-given pleasure.

Election is likewise perceived by some as a subject to be avoided—somewhat pleasant perhaps (because it is in the Bible), but otherwise quite detestable. When actually understood and assessed, however, this doctrine takes on an entirely different taste. It becomes a treasured and satisfying aspect of the believer's praise and worship.

While the Bible clearly supports the concept of election, a number of objections are often raised. I would like to delineate these objections and provide a brief answer to each. The answers can help us glimpse aspects of election that might otherwise pass unnoticed.

The first objection is that election is unfair. This objection calls for two responses. First, it would be perfectly fair for God *not to save anyone*. This is exactly how He responded to the angels who sinned (2 Pet 2:4), and their condemnation was entirely appropriate for a just God to administer. So what we actually see with the doctrine of election is that God is gracious and merciful in offering salvation to anyone at all (Titus 3:4-5). The shoe of unfairness should actually be on the other foot—strictly speaking, it seems unfair for God *to save anyone*.

Second, the fact that God saves some while not saving others does not give His creatures the right to question His wisdom. Paul dealt with this sort of objection in Romans 9:19: "Thou wilt say then unto me, Why doth he yet find fault? For who hath resisted his will?" Evidently, Paul anticipated the objection that God should be deemed unfair because He had ultimately determined each person's destiny. But we must note Paul's response in verses 20-21: "Nay but, O man, who art thou that repliest against God? Shall the thing formed say to him that formed it, Why hast thou made me thus? Hath not the potter power over the clay, of the same lump to make one vessel unto honour, and another unto dishonour?"

God has the right to do as He chooses with His creation. As Wayne Grudem states, "If God ultimately decided to create some creatures to be saved and others not to be saved, then that was his sovereign choice, and we have no moral or scriptural basis on which we can insist that it was not fair."[3]

The second objection is that election contradicts those biblical passages that teach that God wills all to be saved. For example, Paul writes in 1 Timothy 2:4 that God "will have [literally, "wishes"] all men to be saved, and to come unto the knowledge of the truth." Peter states, "The Lord is not slack concerning his promise, as some men count slackness; but is longsuffering to us-ward, not willing that any should perish, but that all should come to repentance" (2 Pet 3:9).

How do these verses mesh with the idea that God only chooses some to be saved? It would appear that the best solution to this dilemma is that these verses speak of God's *revealed* will (i.e., His will of desire) and not God's *hidden* will (i.e., His will of decree). The verses tell us that God invites, desires, and

---

[3]Wayne Grudem, *Systematic Theology* (Grand Rapids: Zondervan, 1994), 683.

commands every person to believe in Christ for salvation, but they do not tell us anything about God's overarching decree regarding who will be saved. There are other occasions in Scripture where God decrees (allows) something to take place that He elsewhere commands not to happen. For example, God wills that Christ be crucified (Acts 2:23) when He clearly forbids murder (Exod 20:13). God wills that the ten kings wage war against the Lamb (Rev 17:16-17) even though it is clearly sinful to do so. God wills that Pharaoh's heart be hardened against Israel (Exod 4:21) even though He commands Pharaoh to let them go (Exod 8:1).[4] Thus, it would appear that God decrees certain things (the salvation of the elect) while commanding seemingly contradictory things (the need for everyone to repent).

I should add here that virtually all truly Christian theologians agree in recognizing God's universal calls for repentance while at the same time admitting that not everyone is saved. Everyone believes that God deems *something* more important than saving everyone. Some (like me) believe that God deems His own glory as more important (Rom 9:22-23) while others believe that God considers the preservation of human free will (understood in libertarian terms) to be supreme. Thus, we can observe the fundamentally distinct ways in which these two approaches understand the nature of God as seen in His providential directing of election.

The third objection is that election eliminates human choice from saving faith. We ought to consider this objection from two perspectives. On the divine level, God ordains that certain people believe in Christ for salvation. Subsumed under that divine decree, however, is the human level where humans make voluntary

---

[4]For a very helpful description of God's two wills, see John Piper, "Are There Two Wills in God?" in *Still Sovereign*, ed. Thomas Schreiner and Bruce Ware (Grand Rapids: Baker, 2000), 107-131.

choices. Viewed from the second perspective, most humans choose to reject the Savior (John 8:44—Ye are of your father the devil, and the lusts of your father ye will [literally, "wish to"] do) for which reason they are "without excuse" (Rom 1:20). On the other hand, people will decide to trust in Christ when God opens their hearts so that they can believe (Acts 11:21; 13:48). In both instances, humans make free choices which produce genuine effects on their lives. Free choice and election are not mutually exclusive concepts. Instead, free choice operates under the authority of God's electing hand.

Like coffee, the doctrine of election may be repudiated by those who have no taste for it. Nevertheless, it ought to be viewed from the perspective of the biblical authors. They see election first of all *as a comfort*. Paul states that God works for the good of those who love Him (Rom 8:28); this comforting assertion finds its basis in the predestining election of God (v. 29). Second, election is presented as a reason to praise God. This truth is presented numerous times (Eph 1:6, 12, 14; 1 Thess 1:2, 4; 2 Thess 2:13). Third, election is presented (surprisingly for some) as an encouragement to evangelism. In 2 Timothy 2:10 Paul states that he endures "all things for the elect's sakes, that they may also obtain the salvation which is in Christ Jesus with eternal glory." For Paul, election is God's guarantee that there will be some success in evangelism, and because of this he is willing to endure suffering.

Far from being a harsh or unpalatable doctrine, election deserves our meditation and appreciation. Once acquired, the believer's taste for this truth will only grow stronger, for it allows one to savor the glory, justice, and mercy of God. Those who hold an accurate understanding of God's purpose in election will be moved to praise and admire Him.

PSALM 73

Translated by Roy Beacham

I am always with you; you have taken hold of my right hand.
With your counsel you guide me again and again, and finally you will
*   receive me to glory.*
Who in the heavens is mine?
And in comparison with you there is nothing on the earth I desire.
My flesh and my heart are spent, but God is the strength of my heart
*   and my portion forever.*
For behold, the ones who depart from you shall perish;
You bring to an end all of those who turn away in unfaithfulness
*   from you.*
But for me, the nearness of God is good for me.
I have made Yahweh God my refuge, so that I might recount all your
*   works.*

MY HAND IN HIS

Roy Beacham

I walk with you,
You hold my trembling hand and guide my way;
I hear your voice,
And listening well I cannot widely roam.
I do not fear,
Your counsel is my surety, guide, and stay;
And in the end,
I find your gracious hand has led me home.

I've naught in heaven
But you, and nothing else I hope to own;
And naught on earth
Could ever cause my passion steal away.
My flesh may fail,
My mortal heart with want might faithless groan;
But you, my strength,
Will be my God, my heart, my all for aye.

All those who walk
Afar from you shall perish, bound in fear;
Whose end is sure,
For lack of faith their destiny they cede.
But as for me,
I find it precious good to walk so near
My refuge strong;
I joy to tell your every wondrous deed.

THREE

Christ Our Savior

ę

COME, LET US ADORE HIM

Kevin T. Bauder

*A*ll Christians at all times and in all places have one thing in common: we worship Jesus Christ. In His presence we feel compelled to bend the knee and bow the head. We cannot escape the feeling that He is worthy, not merely of esteem, respect, and admiration (as if He were simply the greatest of teachers and humanitarians), but rather of adoration, exaltation, and glorification. We worship Jesus Christ, and we long for the day when every knee will bow and every tongue will confess that Jesus Christ is Lord.

When we worship Jesus, we are tacitly acknowledging that He is God. None but God is worthy of worship. Apostles refused worship (Acts 14:14-15). Angels rejected it (Rev 22:8-9). Herod was struck down with worms for accepting worship rather than giving glory to God (Acts 12:22-23). God alone is worthy of worship. He alone merits adoration.

Yet Jesus Christ freely accepted worship. He received worship from the man born blind (John 9:38). He accepted the worship of the disciples who were in the ship when He walked on the water (Matt 14:33). He welcomed adoration from Thomas, who cried out, "My Lord and My God!" (John 20:28). The risen Lord Jesus offered no rebuke to the disciples when they clasped His feet and worshipped Him (Matt 28:9).

In the Revelation, John shows the Lamb being adored along with the Father: "Blessing, and honour, and glory, and power, be unto him that sitteth upon the throne, and unto the Lamb for ever and ever" (Rev 5:13). This is the very worship that every Christian yearns to offer. We long for the day when, finally in the presence of our Lord, we cast ourselves at His feet and wash them with the tears of our joy. We ache to cry out with redeemed hearts and minds and tongues, "Worthy is the Lamb that was slain to receive power, and riches, and wisdom, and strength, and honour, and glory, and blessing!"

Sometimes people express concern that the over-exaltation of the Son might somehow detract from the glory of the Father. They need not worry. Jesus Himself clearly taught that the Father has committed all judgment to the Son, specifically in order that all people would honor the Son just as they honor the Father (John 5:22-23). In other words, the Father delights in the honor and glory of the Son. The Father is most glorified when the Son is most magnified. Every bit of worship that is offered to Christ redounds to the glory of the Father. In fact, no one can worship the Father without worshipping the Son. Son-worship is the mode that the Father has given us to worship Himself.

The way that we worship the Father is by worshipping the Son. This is the case because of the kind of relationship that the Father and Son enjoy with each other. That relationship has no human equivalent.

On the one hand, the Father and the Son are distinct persons. The Father blessed the Son at His baptism. The Son prayed to the Father repeatedly. In Gethsemane, the Son clearly distinguished His will from the will of the Father: "not my will, but thine, be done" (Luke 22:42). Any attempt to erase the distinction of persons reduces these exchanges to a grotesque form of shadow-boxing. Scripture everywhere teaches that the Son is not the Father. They are distinct persons.

On the other hand, the Father and the Son are one God, for there is only one God (Deut 6:4). They are one and the same being, co-equal, co-eternal, and consubstantial. The Son is of one nature (*homoousios*) with the Father. He is not ontologically inferior to the Father, though He did choose to subordinate Himself administratively during His humiliation.

This is the point at which language begins to fail us. We know that both Father and Son are one and the same God, and we know that they are not the same person. Yet we have no experience whatever with distinct persons who are the same being. Our finite lives provide no equivalent for the relationship of Father to Son. Almost every attempt to reason about this relationship is freighted with the risk of heresy. One tiny misstep in either direction and we can end up denying something that is essential to the faith. Whatever we say, we must be careful to maintain both fundamental insights: the Father and Son are not distinct beings, but they are not the same person.

One thing is certain, however. Because the Father and Son are one and the same God, the relationship between them must be far closer and more intimate than the relationship between any two created persons. From all eternity they share each other's being. In their infinite wisdom they know each other's minds with precision. And their relationship is one of infinite, eternal, unsurpassable love.

Scripture describes this relationship by saying that the Father loves the Son. Because of this love, the Father has given all things into the hand of the Son (John 3:35). Because He loves the Son, the Father has completely disclosed His plan to the Son (John 5:20). He publicly declares the Son to be His beloved (Matt 3:17; 17:5). Therefore, the Son declares the Father, displaying the love of the invisible God and making it accessible to human minds (John 1:18; 17:26).

So close is the connection between Father and Son that whoever has seen the Son has also seen the Father (John 14:9).

The Father is like a bright light, and the Son is like the rays that come from the light; the Father is like the image on a die, and the Son is like the image on the coin that is struck by the die (Heb 1:3). That is why every act of worship toward the Son is also an act of worship toward the Father. The Father desires nothing more than that Christ should have the preeminence, because the entire fullness of Deity dwells in the Son in bodily form (Col 1:18-19; 2:9).

With what words shall we confess this? No one has ever improved upon this expression: We believe "in one Lord Jesus Christ, the only-begotten Son of God, begotten of the Father before all worlds; God of God, Light of Light, very God of very God; begotten, not made, being of one substance with the Father, by whom all things were made." Every lover of Jesus Christ thrills to these words. Every pious heart resonates. When we repeat the Creed, it is no vain repetition. Rather, we find ourselves exclaiming, "Yes! This is my Lord Jesus Christ!"

So let us bend our knees and bow our heads before Him. Let our hearts rejoice in Him even as our mouths confess Him. Let us glorify Him and magnify His name. O come, let us adore Him!

CHRIST THE LORD

Kevin T. Bauder

A mediator attempts to bring about reconciliation between two parties. In order to perform this task, mediators must possess one crucial qualification. They must have sympathies for both parties. A mediator whose sympathies are entirely on one side is not a mediator, but an accomplice and conspirator.

A priest is a kind of mediator. Priests represent humans before God, seeking to reconcile the wayward who have violated God's justice. The writer to the Hebrews teaches that compassion for sinning people is one of the qualifications of a priest, particularly a high priest (Heb 5:2-3). In order to gain this compassion, the Levitical high priest had to be one who "wore weakness." Indeed, before he could offer a sacrifice for the sins of the people, he first had to offer a sacrifice for his own sins.

Although such a priest would have obvious sympathy for sinful people, he would lack adequate sympathy for God's holiness. Because the priest was a sinner himself, he could offer no sacrifice that would truly propitiate God and expiate sin. His inadequacy did not consist in the fact that he experienced weakness. The failure was that, in his weakness, the priest himself had sinned. Therefore, he could represent only one side in the dispute. The efficacy of his sacrifice was necessarily limited.

The writer to the Hebrews affirms that Jesus Christ has become the final mediator who represents humans before God. He is our great High Priest. His work was to reconcile humans to God, propitiate God's justice, expiate sins, and redeem sinners through the blood of His cross. There He offered Himself as a once-for-all sacrifice for sins.

The sacrifice of Jesus is wholly efficacious for all believers because He was both like and unlike earthly priests. He was unlike them in that He was the eternal Second Person of the Godhead. Of course He sympathized and identified with God. He was God! He understood the importance of justice, and He determined from eternity past that justice had to be fulfilled. He had no propensity merely to excuse or to overlook sins.

Furthermore, because of His divine nature He did not and could not commit sins. The sacrifice that He offered was the only one ever offered that was utterly pure in itself, offered by a priest who was utterly pure in Himself. Because His sacrifice was backed by the infinite purity of His deity, it was the only sacrifice that could truly remove the infinite guilt of human sin and satisfy the infinite justice of a holy God. If Jesus were not truly God, then He could not be our savior.

On the other hand, Jesus was also like human priests in that He shared their nature and even their weakness. He did not take the nature of angels, but He entered the world as a true human being. The genuine humanness of Jesus is essential to His work as mediator. He could not represent us before God if He did not sympathize with us. For this reason, He had to be made like us in every way (apart from sin) in order that He might become a merciful and faithful High Priest. Therefore, He made the choice to "wear weakness" (Heb 5:2-3) like the Old Testament priests. What does this mean?

It means that, to His deity, the Second Person added a complete human nature. It also means that during the time of His humiliation He "emptied Himself" (Phil 2:7) by receiving the form of a slave and coming to be in the likeness of humans. In His weakness He experienced temptation and grief, manifested human piety, and learned obedience through suffering (Heb 5:7-8).

In order to save us, Jesus had to be one of us. He had to experience the full force of human limitation, frailty, and weakness. He had to be tested, and He had to face testing with the same resources that are available to any human.

We fail to appreciate the utter humanity of Jesus Christ. True, during His humiliation Jesus never ceased to be God and never surrendered any divine attribute. The limitation that He accepted, however, was that He would not use His own divine power unless directed to do so by the Father. As Paul put it, He received the form of a slave (Phil 2:7). His faithfulness, therefore, was the faithfulness of a man, His labor was the labor of a man, and His weakness was the weakness of a man.

What about Jesus' miracles? They were the deeds of the human Messiah, upon whom rested the Spirit of God without measure (John 3:34). This Spirit that God gave to Jesus was the Spirit of the Lord, the Spirit of wisdom and understanding, the Spirit of counsel and might, the Spirit of knowledge and the fear of the Lord (Isa 11:2). This immeasurable, seven-fold Spirit of God (Rev 5:6) imparted such knowledge and ability as Jesus needed in order to perform His messianic wonders. With some exceptions, these wonders seem not to have been the direct manifestation of His own deity, but rather the demonstration of His complete dependence upon His Father through the Spirit.

The Lord Jesus was utterly human, fragile and weak, completely dependent upon His God and Father. In other words, He was exactly what any one of us should have been. Of all humans, Jesus Christ alone has lived a life of genuine, human righteousness, a life of perfect obedience. This active, human obedience constitutes the righteousness of Christ that is imputed to us when we believe.

Jesus no longer experiences humiliation. Since His resurrection and ascension, He has been exalted above the heavens. Our

Brother now governs the universe. He once again receives the adoration of seraphim and cherubim. To the glory of His eternal deity, however, has been added the excellence of a perfect humanity. We worship Him as God, and we also adore Him as the Anointed One.

Though He is now exalted, Jesus has never forgotten what it means to be weak. He never will forget. Precisely because He walked this earth as a fragile human being, experienced testing, passed through suffering, and learned obedience, He is now qualified to be our merciful and faithful High Priest. He is the one mediator between God and humans. He is able to help us when we are tempted. He is able to save us to the uttermost. And for our part, we can come boldly to the throne of grace, knowing that we shall obtain mercy and find help in time of need.

Jesus Christ loves to embrace sinners. He delights to forgive. Before the demands of divine justice, He pleads the merit of His own blood and righteousness. He is our God, our Brother, and our Savior.

O come, let us adore Him: Christ the Lord!

WORD OF THE FATHER, NOW IN FLESH APPEARING

Kevin T. Bauder

If Jesus Christ were not truly and perfectly God, He could not be our mediator. If Jesus Christ were not truly and perfectly human, He could not be our mediator. This much, Scripture makes clear.

Our problem is that we have no experience with divine-human beings other than Jesus Christ. He is absolutely unique, the only one of His kind. For that reason, Christians have struggled to find words to express just who Jesus is.

With the Athanasian Creed we affirm that, as to their deity, the Father and Son are equally glorious, eternal, uncreated, incomprehensible, and almighty. Yet they are not two Gods, but one. So we confess.

Nevertheless, we also confess that we do not comprehend what we affirm. While the relationship of the Father to the Son involves no logical contradiction, it is inexplicable and impenetrable to the human mind. It rises above reason. We do not understand how such a thing can be.

Already bewildered, we then encounter the full humanity of the Son. Here we discover a person who, as to His deity, is co-equal, co-eternal, and consubstantial with God the Father, but who, without ceasing to be fully God, also becomes fully human. We are asked to believe that a person who is equal with God is also one of us.

Not everyone agrees. Often, people reject what they cannot explain. Worse yet, they modify the truth to fit some human explanation. So they have done with the person of Christ.

Some have denied His full deity. Ebionites saw Jesus as a good man, a teacher and prophet who kept the law. Arians explained Jesus as God's first creation, so highly exalted above others that He could be called "a god," but who was still not properly "God." Adoptionists (Dynamic Monarchians) understood Jesus as a human who was elevated to divine status by some act of God.

Some have denied the distinction of the Son from the Father. Sabellians (Modalistic Monarchians) affirmed that Father, Son, and Holy Spirit were simply three modes in which God presented Himself and not actual personal distinctions. As the same man might appear as husband to his wife, as teacher to his students, and as peer to his fellows, God presented Himself at one time as Father, at another as Son, and at another as Holy Spirit. Ultimately, however, the Trinity is a mask, and God is one and only one person.

Others have denied Jesus' complete humanity. Docetists believed that the human body of Jesus was a mere phantom projected by the divine Christ. Apollinarians taught that Jesus possessed a human body and soul, but that the place of the rational, human spirit was taken by the divine Logos (in other words, Christ was 3/3 divine but only 2/3 human). Eutychians affirmed complete divine and human natures, but saw the human nature so recessive as to be almost completely overwhelmed by the divine—rather like a drop of honey in an ocean of water.

Still others have rejected the integrity of the person of Jesus Christ. Cerinthians believed that the divine Christ (a spirit) descended upon the human Jesus, only to abandon Him before the cross. Nestorians affirmed the full deity and full humanity of Christ, but divided these two natures into two distinct persons, joined rather like Siamese twins.

The equal and opposite reaction was for others to affirm the unity of the person by denying the distinctiveness of the natures. Monophysites collapsed the divinity and humanity of Christ into a single nature. In principle this nature was supposed to be both divine and human, but in practice the divine so overwhelmed the human that Monophysitism became a reaffirmation of Eutychianism. A more subtle form of denying the distinction between the natures was Monothelitism, which denied that Jesus had a human will. *De facto*, this constituted a denial of the completeness of the human nature of Jesus.

These are not merely ancient heresies. They have had a tendency to reappear throughout church history. Jehovah's Witnesses are unreconstructed Arians. Mormonism applies Adoptionist principles, not only to Christ, but to all humanity. Many liberals have regarded Jesus simply as a human teacher or prophet, and contemporary biblical scholarship is witnessing a resurgence of interest in Gnostic understandings of Christ. Modalistic Monarchianism shows up in the teachings both of Witness Lee and of the so-called "Jesus Only Movement," represented by the United Pentecostal Church. The Coptic Orthodox Church still defends Monophysitism and condemns the Council of Chalcedon as "divisive."

Our understanding of the person of Christ has been hammered out in opposition to these heresies. Each new heretical theory forced Christians to return to the Scriptures in order to test the theory against the text. At each new controversy, Christians erected a new barrier against heresy. They were forced to say, "Scripture teaches *this* but not *that*. We may say it *this* way but not *that* way." This process resulted in the adoption of several public summary statements, each of which was more specific than the one that preceded it.

At the end of the day, here is what we must affirm. If Jesus Christ were not true God, He could not be our savior. If Jesus Christ were not true human, He could not be our savior. If Jesus Christ were not one person, he could not be our savior. If the person of Christ were divided, then He could not be our savior. If the natures were combined or transmuted, then He could not be our savior. All of this is summarized and elaborated in the formula of Chalcedon.

Nothing is more important to Christianity than the incarnation of Jesus Christ. A false step here can lead us to deny the gospel and plunge us into apostasy. We learn about the old heresies so that we may confront the new ones. We confront the new ones so that we may keep the gospel pure. We aim for precision in our understanding of Jesus Christ so that we may trust Him and worship Him as He is, rather than worshipping a false Jesus whom we have manufactured in our own idolatrous hearts.

In one sense, we are indebted to the heretics. Everything that we need to know about Jesus Christ is in the text of Scripture. If we had not been challenged by the heretics, however, we never would have studied the Scriptures as they deserved to be studied. We never would have noticed the depth and texture and richness of the biblical teaching concerning the incarnation. The heretics have forced us to discover exactly what Scripture says and what it forbids us to say.

We cannot explain the incarnation. We cannot fully comprehend the notion of a theanthropic person. But we can learn to be precise in saying who He is and who He is not. We can know Him. We can trust Him. We can love Him. We can worship Him. Word of the Father, now in flesh appearing: O come, let us adore Him, Christ the Lord.

THE COMPLETENESS OF THE INCARNATION

Kevin T. Bauder

*L*eo Steinberg, writing for *Harper's Magazine* in March of 1984, offered a series of fascinating observations about Domenico Ghirlandaio's *Adoration of the Magi*. The work depicts the Christ child, held by the Virgin, being examined by the wise men. They are gazing in rapt astonishment at the undraped Christ. What Steinberg points out—and what is obvious once noticed—is that the gaze of the Magi is directed toward the child's reproductive organs.

Ghirlandaio's painting is anything but unique. Botticelli conceals the child's genitals from the viewer and permits Him to be examined only by one Magus, but the object of the wise man's gaze is still unmistakable. Filippino Lippi has the child partially exposed to the viewer as well as to the Magi. Paolo Veronese shows the Virgin lifting aside the child's wrap and presenting Him nether-end first to an amazed Magus. In Pieter Aertsen's rendition, the Christ, hand raised in a gesture of blessing, is fully exposed to the viewer while a basket of folded diapers sits by Mary's side. Sebastiano Ricci chooses the moment immediately following the inspection: Mary is replacing the cover over the child, while the aged Magus still peers so closely that the Christ places a hand upon his head.

To be sure, not all paintings of the Magi portray the scene in the same way. Some show the Magi presenting their gifts to the child. Others show one Magus kissing the Savior's foot. Yet others simply depict the Magi in some other act of obeisance.

Nevertheless, enough of these paintings (certainly more than I have listed) show the wise men gazing at the baby's genitals that there can be no mistake—these artists had a lesson they wanted to emphasize.

As a matter of fact, their point is a doctrinal one. Their paintings constitute a theological reflection on the nature and significance of the incarnation. They are telling us something about who the Christ is and what He does.

The point is about the incarnation. By *incarnation* we mean that the Second Person of the Godhead, without ceasing to be God, added to His deity a complete human nature. He took humanity into Himself in such a way that His person is not divided, but also in such a way that the natures are never confounded or converted. The incarnation tells us who Christ is.

Who Christ is relates directly to what Christ does. The story of the incarnation is not an end in itself but an introduction to the great story of sacrifice and redemption. In Christ, God became incarnate not simply to prove that He could, but rather to offer Himself as a sacrifice for our sins. He came as our redeemer, our savior. Christians understand that the incarnation is necessary for our redemption.

An ancient dictum says that Christ can only redeem that in which He participates. He did not take on Him the nature of angels, and therefore He does not redeem angels. He did, however, take the seed of Abraham. Since those whom He wished to redeem were flesh and blood, He had to partake of flesh and blood (Heb 2:14-17). He had to be made like His brothers in order to save them. He had to share their nature.

The question is, How much of human nature does Christ share? In how much humanity does He participate? Gnosticism answered this question by denying that Christ participated in human nature at all. For Gnostics, anything material was evil, and human nature was material, so Christ could not have participated in human nature. Docetists insisted that the human body of Christ was a mere phantom. Cerinthians argued that the divine Christ temporarily came upon the human Jesus. On either account, materiality and humanity were denied.

For Gnostics, the most offensive aspect of human nature was sexual reproduction. Most Gnostics tended to be severe ascetics in many ways, but they were especially ascetic in their view of sexuality. For the average Gnostic, nothing was more degrading to humanity.

While Christianity rejected Gnosticism, certain Gnostic elements occasionally spilled over into Christian sensibility. One of those elements was the distrust of sexuality and especially of sexual pleasure. Formally, medieval theologians such as Thomas Aquinas defended the goodness of sexual pleasure within marriage. Nevertheless, Catholicism displayed a sense that marriage and the bearing of children were somehow inferior to celibacy and virginity. .

The paintings of Ghirlandaio and others are offering a rebuttal to this perspective. The paintings are not about the wise men but about the incarnation. In these paintings, the Magi are astonished at the completeness of the human nature that the Savior has adopted—a nature so entire that it includes reproductive organs. In the incarnation, God did not simply dip His toe into the pool of humanity. On the contrary, He plunged Himself into the fullness of human nature, becoming everything that is naturally human.

The implication is that Christ intended to redeem the entire human nature. Since our humanity includes our sexuality, and since He took up sexuality in the human nature that He assumed, then He must have meant to redeem it. There is a message here, not only about the incarnation, but about God's intention for humanity. God means for humans to "be fruitful and multiply," in accordance with which He created our sexual natures. What God made is good, and what Christ redeems is good. To view marriage and childbearing as inferior to singleness and virginity is to wander into heresy.

A secondary lesson can also be found in these paintings, and it is one that needs to be learned by twenty-first century Christians. The paintings are addressing the misperception of human sexuality. Indeed, they are pointing out the sexuality of Jesus. But they do so in an extremely careful and reverent manner.

This reverence is directed not merely toward Christ, but toward sexuality itself. While sex is a good part of God's creation, it is both powerful and easily twisted. Sexuality can be debased more thoroughly and destructively than almost any other aspect of our humanity. Therefore, it is a subject that must be treated with care.

We find it easy to criticize those Victorians who, out of prudishness, put stockings over the legs of pianos. It is always easy to criticize the sins that we are not being tempted to commit. Modern Christians are no longer prudes. Quite the opposite. We have begun to speak of sexual matters with the contemptuous familiarity and coarse ribaldry that once typified junior high locker rooms. One cringes to think how certain evangelical leaders might handle the topic of Jesus' sexuality.

These artists addressed it with decorum. They employed their skills to make a necessary but sensitive point. They took pains to avoid dishonoring or debasing either the Christ child or the human sexuality that He took into Himself. Their message, subtly conveyed, was nevertheless clear and powerful. Christ became one of us in the most utter and complete sense. Because He identified with us completely, He is able to redeem us completely. These are powerful themes, and we owe a debt to Ghirlandaio and other artists for reminding us of them.

HIS REMARKABLE MOTHER

Kevin T. Bauder

*W*hat a remarkable woman. She was a bride already during her teen years. Exactly when the marriage had been covenanted is uncertain, but she was reckoned as a wife. Her husband was an older man, and he was still waiting (for what? for her to grow up?) before taking her to him. Though husband and wife, they had never lived together, never slept together. She was still a virgin bride.

Her husband was a son of kings. She, too, could trace her family line back to the greatest of the kings of her people. Centuries had passed, however, since any of that king's lineage had worn a crown. A curse had been uttered over one of her husband's ancestors, and every son of the lawful bloodline was barred from the throne.

She was of a different line. She and her husband shared that common ancestor—the great king—but for nearly a thousand years their fathers had built separate houses. Only her husband's house could lawfully rule the kingdom. And the sons of that house were cursed.

So here she was, a granddaughter of a king, betrothed to the son of kings, but living in a backwater of a conquered nation. She exercised none of the prerogatives of royalty, nor did she expect that she ever would. Her husband—this son of kings—was a carpenter, a builder by trade.

Could anything have been further from her mind than an angelic visitation? Yet there he was, an ancient and dreadful presence, greeting her, saying that she was "highly favored" (filled to the bursting-point with God's grace), and pronouncing her "blessed among women." No wonder she paled and trembled.

Yet the appalling magnificence brought astounding news. She had found grace in the eyes of God, he said. She was about to conceive and give birth to a child who would be a most unusual person. He would be called the Son of the Most High. He would be given the throne of the great king. He would rule over the nation, once chosen but now conquered. Furthermore, His kingdom would never end.

So much of this announcement was implausible that it was difficult even to know where to begin. Perhaps the question that she asked was the most obvious. How could a girl who was still a maiden—a virgin child-bride—conceive a son? She was not so naïve as to be ignorant of how babies were produced.

The dreadful eminence offered an answer that really explained very little. The Holy Spirit would come upon her. The power of the Most High would overshadow her. Her child would be called holy, the Son of God. With God, nothing is impossible.

These words contained little explanation. What they made clear, however, is that a miracle would be required. Producing that miracle would be God's business, not hers. Her implied choice was either to permit the miracle or not.

She could have no illusions about the consequences if she said *yes*. Everybody knew where babies came from. Her husband would assume that she had been unfaithful (and he did). Other people would assume the same, or else they would be scandalized that she and her husband had commenced cohabitation without the customary rites. In either case, she could expect public shame.

To say *yes* took enormous courage. It also took enormous faith. Yet she had been filled to bursting with God's grace. She was blessed among women, as her own cousin soon affirmed. At that time, she herself would claim that "all generations will call me blessed."

What would she choose? God must have been preparing her for this moment for her entire life. Her mind was full of Scripture, and she had the soul of a poet. She could grasp unseen possibilities. In that moment, she believed that the Lord would do as He had said. She replied, "Behold the handmaid of the Lord; be it unto me according to thy word."

As the weeks passed, it became obvious that she had indeed conceived. Her husband was on the verge of initiating a divorce when he received his own angelic visitation. Immediately he took her into his home, though he was careful to preserve her virginity. His act effectively claimed the unborn child as his own. This remarkable situation would give the child all the rights of the king's house—but it would also exempt him from the ancestral curse. Amazingly, the child would inherit the bloodline of the great king from his mother, while he received the rights of the royal house from his (_adoptive_ is too mild a word) father.

At the moment, however, the adoptive father and the mother who was great with child were still subjects of a conquering, foreign power. That power demanded that they leave the comforts of their home for the city of their common ancestor, the great king. So leave they did.

They arrived in the city of David to find it brimming with travelers. No lodging could be found at any price. Finally, they had to content themselves with a rough-hewn manger.

Of all the nights! She lay on hard stones, cushioned by whatever garments or straw her husband could find. She had no mother to hold her hand, no sister, no kindly aunt. Only a husband with whom she had never shared a bed.

The pains came, then again, harder and faster. Her breath caught. Tears flowed as flesh tore.

She held the tiny thing in her arms. Fragile fingers clasped hers as she cleansed the wrinkled skin. Did she guess what those tiny hands would do—healing the sick, mixing the clay and giving sight to the blind, rescuing Peter from the heaving sea, bearing the nails of the cross? Her work completed for the moment, she wrapped the babe in swaddling cloths and laid him in the manger.

He was her son, as truly and utterly as any son was born of any mother. Yet He was also the Son of God, God the Son, the eternal Second Person of the Godhead. He was one person in two natures, both divine and human, but only one Jesus Christ.

The bearing of this son placed her in a category of her own. She became something that no other woman ever has been or ever can be. She gave birth, not to a nature, but to a son, a person. Her son was the God-man. Therefore, she and she alone is and will ever be *theotokos*, "God-bearer."

We do not worship her, for God alone deserves our adoration. Yet she was and is highly favored—filled to bursting with God's grace. God Himself has pronounced her blessed. Dare we do less?

How should she be called? Not redemptrix, to be sure, nor mediatrix. What about the handmaid of the Lord? The blessed virgin? The mother of God? Dare we deny her these rightful titles?

We marvel at God's grace in the life of Mary. As we ponder the incarnation of our Lord, we rejoice with Mary's joy. We do not understand the mystery of the incarnation—indeed, we marvel at it. We worship her son, just as the shepherds did on the night of His birth. As for Mary herself—well, what a remarkable woman.

GIVING THANKS WHILE REMEMBERING THE INCARNATION

Kevin T. Bauder

O God of God, O Light of Light, O very God of very God, toward You I cast my mind as the tempest casts waves from the sea. Like breakers upon ancient crags do my small thoughts dash against You and fall back into themselves. In You I find—and fail to fathom—height above height and depth beyond depth, eternal and incomprehensible.

Lover of my soul, You veil Yourself from prying eyes. You hide Yourself from the curious and You rebuff the inquisitive. You hold Your radiance as a precious treasure, not as merchandise to satisfy faithless seekers who peer into the transcendent.

O Alpha and Omega, O Uncreated One, O First and Last: You are the only-begotten Son, of one substance with the Father, begotten before all worlds, begotten but not made. You made all things, both visible and invisible, whether things in heaven, or things on the earth, or things under the earth, whether thrones, or dominions, or principalities, or powers. By You all things consist, for You uphold all things by the word of Your power. You are before them all, and they all are by You and for You and in You.

Divine Poet, creation is Your stanza. Though You are altogether above the things that You have made, yet through Your handiwork You disclose Yourself. In the created world have You shown Yourself. By it do we clearly see invisible mysteries. Throughout Your poem have You spoken a message of eternal power and Godhead. The very skies declare Your praise to every eye. Day speaks to day and night whispers to night, and no ear is deaf to their voice.

Let the whole creation sing to Your glory! Let the fowls of the air and the fishes of the sea, the beasts of the field and the trees of the forest cry out Your praises! Let the sea roar and the fields rejoice in Your presence! Let the mountains tremble at Your majesty and the heavens be afraid under Your dominion!

O Helpless Babe, O Mary's Child, O Immanuel, I bow my heart to You. For me and for my salvation You came down from heaven. Of the substance of the Father, You are very God. Of the substance of Your mother, You are very man. Born in this world, You have taken into Your eternal person a perfect humanity, full and real. To Your unaltered deity have You added a reasonable soul subsisting in human flesh, perfect God and perfect man.

In Your person (indivisible!) and through Your natures (unconverted! unconfounded!) does omnipotence grasp weakness, tranquility embrace sorrow, and immortality own death. Before this impenetrable mystery I stand still. My mind balks. You are a wall that I cannot climb. You are a chasm whose depths I cannot fathom. You are a height shrouded in mist and cloud.

I believe.

I believe.

I believe.

I believe though I do not understand. I believe what I do not understand. I believe in order that I might understand.

Through Your incarnation You reach out to me—Word of the Father, now in flesh appearing. Of the Father's love were You begotten, and in love did You assume my nature. Though You subsisted in the form of God, You considered eternal glory a thing to be ungrasped. You emptied Yourself, coming to be in my likeness. For me You made Yourself a slave. When You were found in fashion as a man, You humbled Yourself to the point of death.

O Lamb of God, O Servant of Jehovah, O Savior of Mankind, how can this be? The death of the cross? Bearing my sins in Your own body on the tree? Made to be sin for me—You, who knew no sin?

Frightful love! Dreadful love! Appalling love! Such love reeks of tears and blood. It rings with thunder and wrath. It overpowers Omnipotence and drives it to a cross. O God! What if this love were to seize me? Where would it take me, and how could I bear it?

Your name is Jealous. You will not serve my gods. I cannot fashion You as I might wish, but must receive You as You are in the unity of Your being. Because You have no parts, I cannot select which part appeals to me. If I choose You, still I cannot choose what You will do with me. You bid me come, bid me bow, bid me trust—and You are beautiful in Your holiness! Yet this holiness too, like a naked sword, warns me and resists me and affrights me until I come without demands.

O Advocate, O Mediator, O Merciful and Faithful High Priest, You are my intercessor. Those wounds that on earth for me did bleed do now plead for me before the Father's face. No law can incriminate, nor can any accuser recriminate. My guilt has been charged once-for-all, and once-for-all credited is Your righteousness.

You are my shield and my hiding place. Over Your head broke the storm of divine wrath once; now, safety and peace dwell under the shadow of Your brow. The Hand whose justice smote and crushed at the cross is now the Hand from whose refuge none can pluck. Neither death, nor life, nor angels—You hold me firm, hold me fast, hold me secure. Nor principalities nor powers—You swear that I am Yours. Nor things present, nor things to come—forever have You claimed me. Nor height, nor depth, nor any other creature—this oath, this consolation, this hope, this expectation I find in You alone.

O Alpha and Omega, O Faithful and True, O KING OF KINGS AND LORD OF LORDS, Your day draws near. Soon shall the legions of heaven gather in Your train. From thence shall You return to judge the quick and the dead. You shall tread out the winepress of the fierceness and wrath of Almighty God. You will be revealed from heaven in flaming fire with mighty angels, taking vengeance upon those who know not God.

You are the comfort for which my heart yearns. You are the justice for which my soul hungers and thirsts. With the gladness of Your presence shall I gird myself. You are my portion, my inheritance, and my reward. My heart and flesh cry out, not for Your gifts, but for Yourself. As the swallow seeks its nest, so my soul seeks You.

O Savior, I thank You.

O Christ, I bless You.

O Lord Jesus, I praise You.

May the meditation of my heart be acceptable in Your sight, O Lord, my Strength, and my Redeemer. Worthy is the Lamb that was slain to receive power, and riches, and wisdom, and strength, and honor, and glory, and blessing. As it was in the beginning, is now, and ever shall be, world without end. Amen.

FOUR

Sin and Salvation

ℰ

IS THE WILL TRULY FREE?

Jonathan Pratt

*R*obots play a fascinating role in our technologically advanced world. Astronauts, treasure hunters, and manufacturers would all agree that robots enable them to achieve far more than they could alone. But there are some things robots will never be asked to do because they are incapable of rational thought. They do not possess a will of their own. This is where humans and robots are different. Unlike robots, humans have free will, the power to choose to perform or not to perform an action. Or so it would seem.

Gregory Boyd describes free will this way: people "originate their own actions," and "they are the final explanation for what they choose to do."[5] Thus, the *ultimate* explanation for someone's choosing as he does is his own free will, not God's will or anyone else's. While some might not phrase their understanding of free will in quite the same way, they still would assert that human beings freely make their own choices. To take away this basic fact of human nature would presume that humans are robots, that they are fatalistically bound to do the things that God has pre-programmed them to do.

The type of freedom described by Boyd is known as *libertarian freedom*, and it is the kind of freedom most people (believers and unbelievers alike) refer to when they speak of free will. In contrast, *compatibilist freedom* perceives the predestinating work of God in combination with the voluntary acts of humans so that people freely choose to do actions that God ultimately ordained to occur. In this alternate conception of freedom, humans are morally responsible for freely-chosen actions that God in His

---

[5]Gregory Boyd, *Is God to Blame?* (Downers Grove, IL: IVP, 2003), 70.

wisdom has predestined (Acts 2:23—notice that *wicked* people put Jesus to death but that God purposed the event to take place).

Which of these two conceptions of freedom is the most biblical? Perhaps it would be helpful to answer this question by offering several observations about human existence. These observations illustrate the limitations of our free will.[6]

1) We had no choice in deciding whether or not we would enter this world. Our parents clearly made that determination for us. 2) The nature of the world we invaded was not given to us as an option. We might have preferred a nonmaterial world or a world of pure mind or spirit, but we are stuck with a life that is at least partially physical. 3) We had no say in our ethnicity. 4) The economic status of our family was out of our control. 5) Others chose the country of our birth for us. 6) Those people who influenced our lives—parents, teachers, relatives, friends, colleagues—have shaped us into the people we have become; here, too, our freedom to avoid or embrace such influences has been limited, in part, by them. 7) We have entered a society full of laws and customs that are not our choosing. We may decide to break or to keep them, but we still live with society's sanctions when we break them and with society's approval when we obey. These responses by society are likewise things we do not have freedom to control. 8) Even something like artistic creativity is limited. Artists can only work with tools that already exist in the universe or by human manufacture. God created out of nothing by the word of His mouth. We lack the freedom, omniscience, omnipotence, and wisdom to come close to His handiwork. Here again, we are not entirely free

---

[6]Many of these observations come from Geoffrey Bromiley, "Only God is Free," *Christianity Today* 46, no. 2 (4 February 2002): 72-75.

to create anything we might conceive in our minds. Geoffrey Bromiley exclaims: "Cocreators? No. At very best subcreators!"[7] Many other examples of limitations to our freedom could be given. But these suffice to show that human beings are not nearly as free as many would like to think. And I have yet to mention the greatest detriment to human freedom: depravity. The Bible proclaims that sin has affected the entire human race (Rom 3:9-12, 23); that sin has corrupted every part of our being (Jer 17:9; 1 Cor 2:14; Titus 1:15); and that no one is capable of doing any spiritual good before God (Isa 64:6; John 8:34; Eph 2:1-3; Col 2:13a). The biblical meaning of depravity has huge implications in the discussion about free will because the sinner has no ability to choose righteousness. Paul describes the sinner's situation as one of enslavement to sin (Rom 6:17, 20) and of being under the control of the flesh (Rom 7:5). The ramification of this reality in regard to the most important decision in life (What will you do with Jesus?) spells doom for every member of the human race. The depraved person has no freedom to choose Christ (Rom 3:11) and, in fact, will always choose against Christ unless God graciously draws the sinner to Himself (John 6:44, 65; Eph 2:4-9; Col 2:13b).

John Wesley recognized this problem with depravity and free will, and it led him to espouse the doctrine of "preventing" (we would now say *prevenient*) grace. This doctrine suggests that God counters the effects of depravity by giving everyone the ability to choose Christ. Wesley argued that "everyone has, sooner or later, good desires" that enable them to accept Christ.[8] We can see this belief clearly stated in his sermon entitled "The General Spread of the Gospel." Wesley states, "I am persuaded

---

[7]Bromiley, 74.

[8]John Wesley, "Working Out Our Own Salvation," sermon in *The Works of Wesley*, vol. 6 (Grand Rapids: Baker reprint edition, 1978), 512.

every child of God [every human being] has had, at some time, 'life and death set before him,' eternal life and eternal death; and has in himself the casting vote."[9] Wesley's argument is very logical, but he fails to garner any biblical evidence for this doctrine. Indeed, there is no verse in the Bible that supports Wesley's concept of "preventing" grace.

In light of these observations, we are compelled to deny the reality of libertarian freedom. And in regard to the most important decision people must make, e.g., the destiny of their souls, only one choice is available for the sinner apart from the saving grace of God, and it is the choice that results in eternal separation from God.

Humans do possess free will, but it is compatibilist freedom. It is a freedom that makes willing choices which have real effects (the people who put Christ to death were evil and freely chose to execute him—Acts 2:23; 4:27), but it is always under the ultimate control of God's providential directing ("the determinate counsel and foreknowledge of God," Acts 2:23; "both Herod, and Pontius Pilate, with the Gentiles, and the people of Israel, were gathered together, For to do whatsoever thy hand and thy counsel determined before to be done," Acts 4:27b-28).

In regard to the free choices of humans, compatibilist freedom suggests two realities. For the unbeliever, righteous actions approved by God will never be possible; those in this group face a damning limitation to their freedom. On the other hand, Christians experience the blessing of liberty from sin's domination (Rom 6:6, 7, 18, 22), and they understand what "free will" truly entails. No longer are Christians bound to the enslaving effects of their depravity; they can (and will) choose to be righteous. This is the type of freedom Jesus describes in John 8:36: "If the Son therefore shall make you free, ye shall be free indeed."

---

[9]Wesley, "The General Spread of the Gospel," *Works*, vol. 6, 281.

EATING CHRIST

Kevin T. Bauder

*A*mong those who perceive the bodily presence of Christ in the elements of the communion service, John 6 is sometimes considered to be the decisive word. They see it as the definitive proof text that irrefutably demonstrates that the body and blood of Jesus are present in the Eucharistic elements. They insist that in the Eucharist, people actually eat Jesus' flesh and drink Jesus' blood (John 6:53-56).

Is that really what the passage teaches? If not, then what does it teach? These questions deserve an answer that is firmly grounded in the text.

The early part of John 6 narrates the story about Jesus feeding five thousand men (the text does not say whether women or children were present). This story includes the so-called "miracle of the loaves" in which Jesus multiplies a few loaves of bread to be able to feed an entire multitude.

In view of the miracle, the crowd tried to take Jesus and force Him to become their king, probably because they saw an opportunity for free meals. Jesus, however, slipped away quietly. When evening came, the disciples took boats and began to row to the other side of the Sea of Galilee. When they were hindered by weather, Jesus performed His miracle of walking out to the boat across the water. The story ends with their boat arriving suddenly, and apparently miraculously, near Capernaum.

Meanwhile, the crowd was trying to decide what had happened to Jesus. They saw the disciples leave, and they knew that Jesus was not with them. They waited for a while, but when they discerned that Jesus was gone, they decided to follow the disciples. They took boats and came to Capernaum, where they found Jesus and the disciples. Perplexed, they asked Jesus, "Rabbi, when did you get here?"

Jesus ignored their question. Knowing that the crowd consisted mainly of day-laborers (people who would do a day's work for a day's food), He told them to stop working for "food that perishes," but to work for food that "remains to eternal life." His point was that feeding the body does not satisfy the hunger of the soul, and the feeding of the soul is the more important of the two. These people were so impressed when they were given a free meal that they had followed Jesus across the Sea of Galilee—they were indeed laboring for the food that perishes. Jesus, however, wanted them to exhibit as much concern for their eternal wellbeing as for their temporal satisfaction.

In response to Jesus' statement, the crowd asked a question: "What shall we do that we may work the works of God?" This question implies that they understood their relationship with God to be defined by the works that they would do. If they could do enough of the right things, God would be impressed.

Jesus' reply exposed their misunderstanding. He stated that the "work" that God wanted from them was simply to believe on the one whom God sent. Obviously, this was no work at all, at least not in the sense that they were thinking. It was also a messianic claim on Jesus' part. Indeed, He had already made such a claim when He said that the "Son of Man" (a messianic title) was the one who would give them food that would remain to eternal life.

Jesus was confronting the crowd with His personal claims. These claims were two in number. First, Jesus was claiming to be the Messiah. Second, He was claiming to have the authority to save (as the one who distributes bread that remains to eternal life). Belief in Him was the only thing that God required.

The crowd responded to these claims by asking for a sign. Their request was astonishing in its effrontery. This was the same crowd that had already witnessed the miracle of the loaves. It was the same crowd that had tried to force Him to become king. Now, in reaction to His claims, the people suddenly reversed themselves and insisted upon a sign. Their demand was tantamount to a confession of unbelief.

The crowd, however, did not stop there. Having as good as professed their unbelief, the people went on to specify the kind of sign that they would find convincing: "Our fathers ate manna in the wilderness—he gave them bread out of heaven." Amazingly, these people were angling for more free meals. They were trying to manipulate Jesus into acting like the kind of Messiah they wanted, rather than the Messiah whom God sent Him to be.

In order to expose their duplicity, Jesus lured the crowd on. He stated that the manna given by Moses was not the real bread out of heaven. There was something better than manna, something that came down out of heaven, something that was true bread from God.

The crowd was still thinking in terms of free meals. They understood everything that Jesus said in terms of temporal hunger and temporal eating—just as Jesus knew they would. As He expected, they responded, "Evermore give us this bread!" Their request could be paraphrased, "Yes! Give us the real stuff!"

At this point, Jesus had the crowd exactly where He wanted them. The stage was now set for the confrontation which unfolds in the following verses. In order to understand that confrontation, the following points must be kept in mind.

First, Jesus has drawn a contrast between temporal hunger and eternal hunger, between the needs of the body and the needs of the soul. A meal can satisfy the body, but the soul needs something more. The soul needs eternal life.

Second, Jesus wants people to be as concerned about their eternal needs as they are for their temporal needs. He does not simply dismiss or ignore the needs of the body—after all, He has just fed five thousand men miraculously. He does insist, however, that the needs of the soul are more important. A time will come when the needs of the body will no longer be an issue, but the needs of the soul last forever.

Third, Jesus claims that only God can satisfy the hunger of the soul. Only God provides food that remains to eternal life. To feast with God and to enjoy His company is the very thing that will feed the soul. Joining that feast is the most important thing that any soul can do.

Fourth, Jesus defines the central issue as faith, and, specifically, as faith *in Him*. He is the sole distributor of the food that remains to eternal life. To receive that food means to believe on Him. This is the crucial issue: for Jesus, eating equals believing. Trusting Him is precisely what it means to eat the bread that comes down from heaven. This is a point that Jesus will emphasize in the coming verses.

* * *

To return to the narrative, Jesus has set up a confrontation with the crowd, which was attempting to manipulate Him into becoming the provider for their *material* needs. In return, Jesus encouraged them to attend to their *spiritual* needs, implying that He was the Messiah who could meet those needs. Faced with this claim, the crowd demanded a sign. Alluding to the nature of the sign that they wanted, they said, "Our fathers ate

manna in the wilderness—he gave them bread out of heaven."
Jesus knew that they were looking for another free meal, so
He replied that Moses did not give them the real bread. Jesus
claimed that He could offer better bread, bread that comes down
out of heaven, bread that gives life to the world. The crowd took
the bait, exclaiming, "Evermore give us this bread!"

That was exactly the reaction that Jesus had anticipated,
and His reply went straight to the heart of the matter. "I am
the bread of life," He declared. "The one who comes to me will
never hunger, and the one who believes on me will never thirst."
That was certainly not the kind of bread for which the crowd
was angling.

Jesus had already used the metaphor of eating. He acknowledged
that there is a temporal food for the nourishment of the body,
but He pointed out that food for the soul is more important.
The spiritual food is received by believing on the One whom
God sent. In Jesus' metaphor, eating stands for believing. Bread
stands for Him, and He is to be received or "eaten" by believing
His claims and trusting Him.

When Jesus presented Himself as the "bread of life," He
was strengthening this analogy. His emphasis was clearly on
inner reception of His person and claims: anyone who comes
to Him will never hunger, and anyone who believes on Him
will never thirst. In the metaphor, to eat is to believe.

Without waiting for a reply, Jesus leveled an accusation
against the crowd. "You have seen me," He said, "and you do
not believe." This flat charge of unbelief was justified by the
crowd's insistence upon a sign, when in fact Jesus had already
given them as many signs as they needed. After all, the question
was not whether they were willing for Him to be king. That
was just what they wanted! The question was what kind of a
king He would be. They wanted a king who would care for the

needs of their stomachs. He insisted upon being a king who would address the hunger of their souls, and He demanded that they trust Him. That trust is precisely what they were not willing to grant.

Therefore, Jesus accused His hearers of unbelief. He followed that accusation with a description of their spiritual condition. "All that the Father gives me shall come to me," He said. The implication was that, since they had not come, they were not given to Him by the Father.

If they had come (that is, if they had believed Jesus, i.e., eaten the bread of life), then He would never, ever cast them out. Indeed, His whole purpose was to do the will of the One who sent Him, namely, God the Father. What was the Father's will? "That of all that he has given me, I should lose none of it, but should raise it up again in the last day."

The passage invites the reader to view salvation from two perspectives. Viewed from the divine perspective, God gives certain people to Jesus. These all (without exception) come to Him in saving faith. When they come, He never casts them out and He never loses them. In the last day, He raises them up (a reference to ultimate blessedness).

On the other hand, viewed from the human perspective, some people behold the Son and believe on Him. These people receive eternal life. Jesus promises that He Himself will raise them up in the last day (a reference to ultimate blessedness).

This part of the conversation contains fascinating hints that we can use to shape our ideas about the relationship between divine appointment and human responsibility. Within the text, however, one of the main foci is upon the necessity of faith. Whether viewed from the divine perspective or from the human perspective, faith is part of the picture. No one receives the benefits either of eternal life or of ultimate resurrection without coming to Jesus and believing on Him.

Jesus' listeners had refused to believe. To use the terms of Jesus' metaphor, they had refused to taste the bread of life, without which they had no hope of spiritual nourishment or eternal life. Since they had not come to Jesus or believed in Him, they had no reason to expect Him to raise them up in the last day.

Throughout this conversation, Jesus made assertions that were astonishing. He presented Himself as the one who came down from heaven, as the Messiah, as the giver of life, and as the one who possessed authority to raise the dead. Since His audience did not believe Him, it is not surprising to find them grumbling about His claims.[10]

A major key to this passage lies in the point of their grumbling. Their objection was not about Jesus' metaphor of bread, which they apparently understood. Their objection was rather to His claim that He Himself was the bread, i.e., that He was the one who came down from heaven. They worded their objection with precision: "Isn't this Jesus, the son of Joseph, whose father and mother we know? How does He now say, *I came down from heaven*?" To affirm Jesus' heavenly origin took more credulity than the crowd was able or willing to muster.

Why was it so hard for these people to believe on Jesus? According to their statement, the problem lay in Jesus' human relatedness. His human mother and (supposed) father were well known. This crowd knew where babies came from, and

---

[10]There is a question as to whether at this point Jesus is still addressing the original crowd, or whether the focus shifts to the Jewish leadership in Capernaum. John's text is not entirely clear. While I am taking the addressees as the original crowd, the other interpretation is possible. Neither understanding alters the point of the passage.

it wasn't from heaven. From their point of view, Jesus was just another man—just an ordinary guy. Given their assumptions, Jesus' claims were simply too extravagant to be considered.

Throughout the conversation, the crowd's attitude toward Jesus was hardening. Initially, they wanted to make Him a king. Faced with His claims, though, they first attempted to manipulate Him and then blatantly rejected Him. This patent rejection set the stage for further assertions by Jesus. Those assertions, however, grow out of the preceding context. To understand the rest of the conversation, we must keep in mind several factors.

First, spiritual needs are more important than bodily needs. Just as bread meets the needs of the body, Jesus (the bread of life) is able to meet the needs of the soul. He is the means of life, and He is the one with authority to raise the dead.

Second, eating is a metaphor for believing. To eat Jesus as the bread of life is to acknowledge the truth of His claims and to trust Him. Only by trusting Jesus can one gain the benefits that He offers.

Third, Jesus' spiritual claims seem extravagant when viewed through the humble origins of His humanity. His incarnation (i.e., His enfleshment) is the main obstacle to belief in His spiritual claims. He was a tangible, palpable man of flesh who was born in a manger. Who, then, would believe that He could be the one who came down from heaven? That problem is at the heart of this conversation.

* * *

Jesus' conversation with the crowd revolved around three questions. The first question was, "What sign do you give?" That question was tantamount to a rejection of Jesus' messianic claims. It turned into a crass attempt to manipulate Him into satisfying the appetites of the crowd. Jesus, however, refused to offer another sign. Instead, He rebuked the crowd for their unbelief. He insisted that He had come down from heaven, and that He Himself held authority to raise the dead in the last day.

This claim led to the crowd's second question: "How can He say that He came down from heaven?" The question underscores the unbelief of the crowd. Evidently the people understood what Jesus was claiming, but they could not accept His heavenly origin.

Jesus did not answer the question directly. Rather, He pointed out that no one had the ability to come to Him unless they were drawn by the Father. Those who did come, Jesus promised to raise up in the last day. Clarifying what it meant to be drawn by the Father, Jesus stated that absolutely everyone who heard and learned from the Father would come to Him. In other words, to be drawn by the Father is to hear and learn from the Father. No one comes until drawn in this way, but everyone who is drawn in this way does come.

What does it mean to come to Christ? Jesus equated this coming with believing: "I tell you the absolute truth: the one who believes has eternal life." To come to Jesus and to believe on Him are the very same act.

Coming and believing are also equivalent to "eating the bread." At this point, Jesus returned to the analogy with which He had begun the conversation. Material bread could serve the needs of the body, but the hunger of the soul required spiritual bread. Jesus insisted that He Himself was the bread that would nourish the soul. Anyone who ate this bread (i.e., believed on Jesus or came to Him) would never die, but would live forever.

So far, this was only what the crowd had already heard. Now, however, Jesus introduced a new element. He stated, "The bread that I shall give for the life of the world is my flesh."

This answer had to be difficult for the crowd. The reason that they had trouble believing Him in the first place was because of His flesh, i.e., His material body. As a man of flesh He had identifiable parents and an identifiable origin, or so the crowd thought. His "enfleshment" (His incarnation) was the problem. But now Jesus was insisting that the giving of His flesh was essential for the life of the world. If the crowd was mystified before, this claim must have seemed impenetrable.

The fact is, however, that only an incarnate Jesus could save sinners. For sins to be forgiven, God's justice had to be propitiated. Propitiation required a vicarious sacrifice. A vicarious sacrifice required a body (specifically, a human body). Therefore, when Messiah came into the world, He said, "You [God] did not desire sacrifice and offerings, but you have prepared a body for me" (Heb 10:5). Only through the offering of the body of Jesus have we been made holy once for all (Heb 10:10).

A purely spiritual Jesus would never have been able to suffer and to die in our place. A purely spiritual Lord could never have offered Himself as a sacrifice for our sins. A purely spiritual Christ could never have become our savior. In order to redeem us, the Lord Jesus Christ had to offer His body—His flesh—on the cross of Calvary.

To believe on Jesus means to believe on Him as the God-man, the theanthropic person. When we come to Jesus, we believe on Him as one who was born with a mortal body and who actually died in our place. He is the bread of life, not merely because He is the eternal Second Person of the Godhead, but also because He is the human Jesus who could suffer mortal injury. If we are going to receive Him (i.e., to "eat the bread"), we must believe on the body of His humiliation as well as the divine nature of His glory. The humiliation and mortality of His body are precisely the means through which He accomplished our redemption. His flesh is the bread that we must believe in if we are to receive the eternal life that He purchased through His sufferings.

Jesus' flesh is our bread. His flesh suffered and was crucified. His flesh died and was raised up again. We receive His flesh and make it our bread, not by physically masticating some material substance, but by believing on Him in the totality of His person and work. The bread of life is received and becomes the life of the soul through faith in Jesus.

Consequently, Jesus told the unbelieving crowd, "The bread that I shall give for the life of the world is my flesh." The crowd responded with incredulity. They asked, "How is this man able to give us his flesh to eat?"

In context, the crowd would have understood the reference to Jesus' flesh as a metaphor. From the beginning of His argument with the multitude, Jesus had used the eating of bread to symbolize belief in Him. He repeatedly challenged the crowd with significant claims. He claimed to be the bread that came down from heaven. He claimed to have authority to raise up the dead. He claimed to be sent from God, and He applied a messianic title to Himself. Jesus insisted that anyone who believed on Him would be given eternal life.

The only element that Jesus now added to these claims was that His flesh or body would be the bread that He would give for the life of the world. In other words, Jesus asserted that He was not merely a spiritual, divine savior, but also a very human, incarnate one. His body or flesh—His humanity—would be absolutely essential to our salvation.

If the crowd was following Jesus' metaphor of eating as believing, then they should have understood this claim. They were supposed to believe on Jesus as one who would give His body as a sacrifice for their sins. Nevertheless, understanding the metaphor was no guarantee that they would necessarily accept Jesus' claims.

In fact, they did not believe. Instead, they asked, "How is this man able to give us his flesh to eat?" The thrust of this question was consistent with other questions that the crowd had asked. They simply could not accept the notion that "this man," Jesus, could actually deliver what He claimed to offer.

Jesus, however, refused to retreat. He replied, "I tell you the absolute truth: if you do not eat the flesh of the Son of Man and drink His blood, you do not have life in you. The one who crunches my flesh and drinks my blood has eternal life, and I will raise him up in the last day. For my flesh is true eating, and my blood is true drink. The one who crunches my flesh and drinks my blood remains with me, and I with him. Just as the living Father sent me, and I live because of the Father, also the one who crunches me, that one shall live because of me. This is the bread that came down from heaven, not just as the bread that the fathers ate and died; the one who crunches this bread shall live forever."

Rather than abandoning the metaphor of eating, Jesus intensifies it. Rather than using the generic term "eat," He switches to the word "crunch," a word that designates the act of chewing. Why did Jesus make this switch?

The answer is that the expression "to crunch someone's bread" functioned as an idiom in the Greek of the first century. To "crunch bread" was to be a companion of the one whose bread was crunched. The expression is used in just this way in John 13:18. It designates companionship and fellowship.

Since Jesus had already said that His body was the bread that He would give for the life of the world, the application of the idiom is clear. The body that Jesus gave for us on the cross is the basis of our fellowship with Him. There is no companionship or fellowship with Christ apart from His body. We cannot believe on Christ while rejecting His true humanity, materiality, and incarnation.

Perhaps it is no accident that the first of the great Christological heresies—Gnosticism—attacked just this point. Both Docetists and Cerinthians believed in a divine Christ who was not the human Jesus. In their theology, the Christ could not have had a genuinely human body. His body was either a phantom (Docetism) or else the body of a completely different person temporarily inhabited by the Christ spirit (Cerinthianism).

On the contrary, Jesus Himself insisted emphatically that His material body was essential to our salvation. To believe on Him is exactly to believe in His humanity, His body, His incarnation, and His death. To "crunch bread" with Jesus necessarily has to involve "crunching" His body.

To crunch the body of Jesus and to drink His blood means to believe on Him as the incarnate God and the divine-human Savior. This belief is more than a mere, intellectual acceptance of His claims. It is a trusting dependence in which we cast ourselves upon Him and look to Him alone for salvation. If we believe on Him (crunch His body and drink His blood), Jesus says that we will remain with Him and He with us—another idiom for companionship.

The discourse of John 6 is not about the Eucharist. It is about saving faith. In this discourse, Jesus asserts that He alone has the power to give us eternal life. His gift of life depends upon His body and blood. We cannot come to Him simply as the solution to our temporal needs. We must trust Him as the incarnate one who came down from heaven, as the one who gave His body and shed His blood for us. We must embrace

Jesus in the fullness of His deity and in the fullness of His humanity. We must look to Him as the sacrifice for our sins. He is the one who gave His body, and He is the one with the right to administer forgiveness. Most of all, He is the one who can satisfy the eternal hunger of our souls.

ASSURANCE SECURED ON THE BRIDGE OF PERSEVERANCE

Jonathan Pratt

*W*e had heard the horror stories, but now we were seeing them played out right before our eyes. "Did you hear that Bobby Dalland flunked?" The news spread like wildfire. This was supposed to be a great day of rejoicing as the free and easy days of summer were beckoning us to the ball diamond and the beach. But now our thoughts were clouded by a great uneasiness—could it happen to me? Did I pass or am I going to have to relive fourth grade all over again? Fear gripped me as I hastily opened my report card and skipped right over the important things (like the grades) on the inside of the report; I flipped it over to the back where the "Grade for Next Year" blank was located. What a sense of relief passed over me as I saw the number "5" there. A sense of assurance is a beautiful thing!

Believers also appreciate a sense of certainty about their futures. They seek to be assured in their own hearts that heaven and Jesus and glory are all theirs. If it were possible, believers would like to hold that report card stamped "Heaven" in the "Eternal Destiny" blank. But this scenario does not exist. And this lack of concrete, black-and-white assurance causes some Christians to struggle throughout their earthly lives, often wondering whether or not they belong to Christ. Questions enter their minds quite frequently: "Would a true Christian really be able to commit the sin I just committed?" "Why don't I feel saved today?" "Is it possible that I didn't really accept Christ back when I thought I did?"

No Christian needs to struggle with these kinds of doubts, but, sadly enough, many do. Those who doubt are often thwarted in their service for God, their ministry to others, and in their personal spiritual growth. Others respond to this lack of assurance by getting "saved" over and over again ("just to make sure"). Still others may try to become "super saints," seeking assurance by being extra busy in doing good works. What does the Bible say about assurance? What can help people like these who flounder to stay afloat on the tempestuous sea of doubt?

Three foundational concepts need to be clarified in defining assurance. First, *security* is the objective (biblical) guarantee of eternal salvation for all who believe in Jesus. Simply put, God promises that salvation can never be lost (John 10:27-29; Eph 1:13-14; 2 Cor 1:20-22; 5:5). Second, *perseverance* is the enabling that God provides for all true believers to continue in faith and good works. Every true Christian produces righteous fruit (John 15:16; Eph 2:10; Phil 1:6). Third, *assurance* is the subjective awareness of the believer that relates to his personal knowledge and certainty of eternal salvation. It is a kind of personal intuition, both mental and emotional (Rom 8:16; Heb 6:11; 10:22; 1 John 2:3; 5:13).

How does assurance relate to security and perseverance? In a nutshell, perseverance is the bridge between security and assurance. On one side of the chasm, Scripture clearly affirms that no one can ever lose salvation once God has provided it. But on the other side stands one's personal assurance of that reality. How can I *feel* what the Scripture so clearly *asserts*? The answer to this enigma and the bridge across this chasm is perseverance. Many, however, misunderstand what the doctrine of perseverance signifies. So before answering our initial question about assurance, we must grasp the meaning of perseverance.

Thankfully, the Bible contains numerous references to perseverance. Jesus and the New Testament writers describe

Christians who persevere in good works. First, Jesus uses the metaphor of fruit-bearing to describe perseverance. In the parable of the sower, the good ground produces good crops (Matt 13:23; Mark 4:20; Luke 8:15). Jesus is the vine and His branches (His children) bear fruit (John 15:2, 5, 8, 16). Good trees (believers) bear good fruit (Matt 7:17; 12:33; Luke 6:43-45). Second, Paul suggests that Christians will persevere by living obediently (Rom 7:6; 8:28; 2 Cor 9:8; Eph 2:10), by having a new perspective (2 Cor 5:16), and by having new desires (Rom 6:21; Phil 2:13; Titus 2:14). Third, Peter uses some of the same ideas as Paul to talk about perseverance when he states that Christians rejoice in their salvation (1 Pet 1:6, 8; Rom 5:11), love God (1 Pet 1:8; Rom 8:28), and live obediently (2 Pet 1:5-11; Rom 7:4). Fourth, John gives three tests by which we can judge whether or not someone is a persevering Christian: he keeps God's commandments (1 John 2:3-6; 2:28-3:10), loves his Christian brothers and sisters (1 John 3:11-18; 4:7-21), and confesses Jesus as the Messiah (1 John 2:20-23; 4:1-3; 5:6-7).

The New Testament writers also describe perseverance by making conditional statements about the destiny of Christians. While these may appear to imply that a Christian might lose his salvation, they are intended to show evidences of perseverance. Jesus said, "*If* ye continue in my word, then are ye my disciples indeed" (John 8:31). "And you...hath he reconciled in the body of his flesh through death...*if* ye continue in the faith grounded and settled" (Col 1:21-23). "For we are made partakers of Christ, *if* we hold the beginning of our confidence stedfast unto the end" (Heb 3:14). "They went out from us, but they were not of us; for *if* they had been of us, they would no doubt have continued with us" (1 John 2:19).

Another way that the New Testament emphasizes perseverance is by means of warnings against false faith. Paul tells his readers that they must remember the gospel and hold firmly to it because if they do not, they will have believed in vain (1 Cor 15:1-2). The writer of Hebrews issues five specific warnings interwoven throughout his epistle (2:1-4; 3:7-4:11; 5:12-6:20; 10:26-39; 12:15-29); on my view, each warning suggests that the readers will not escape eternal punishment if they fail to persevere. At the end of Revelation, John warns his readers that they face removal from the holy city (i.e., damnation) if they take away from the words of the book (Rev 22:19).

To summarize, the New Testament clearly affirms that true Christians will continue and progress in faith and good works. The conditional promises and warnings should not be causes for doubt but rather encouraging reminders of God's grace to His children as He seeks to urge them on in faith and obedience. True believers can rest assured in the promise that God will enable His children to persevere.

How do these observations relate perseverance to assurance? I began by seeking to provide hope for the doubting Christian. And after investigating the biblical material related to the doctrine of perseverance, I believe we have all we need to help in creating the bridge from security to assurance. Simply, the best proof we have of our eternal security is our perseverance. Paul was not afraid to encourage self-examination in this regard (2 Cor 13:5). He was not encouraging investigation of past prayers or subjective feelings. He was suggesting that one examine his own perseverance. Am I bearing fruit as a Christian (Luke 6:43-45)? Do I show evidence of Christian virtues (2 Pet 1:5-7)? Do I love my fellow brothers and sisters in Christ (1 John 4:7-21)? None of these questions demands that we answer "Yes, 100% of the time I am obedient!" Rather, these questions get to the heart of what it means to be a child of God. Do we care about obedience because God does? Do we long to please our Heavenly Father? Do we want to love and serve Him? Unbelievers cannot answer these questions in the affirmative, but true believers must.

Next to perseverance stand two more points of hope for doubters. First, the inward testimony of the Holy Spirit in the life of the individual believer serves to confirm his standing as God's child (Rom 8:16). While this is a subjective proof, it is certainly a welcome comfort to all God's heirs who enjoy the indwelling, regenerating ministry of the Spirit. Second, the clear statements of the Bible provide believers with assurance that those who call on the Lord will be saved (Rom 10:13) and that those who call are eternally secure (John 10:27-29).

So, unlike my fellow fourth graders and me, who were so uncertain about making it to fifth grade, the Christian has nothing to doubt. God has promised that He will help us to persevere. This persevering obedience is what gives Christians the best evidence of their security in Christ. When we add the indwelling testimony of the Spirit and the rock-solid assurances of God's Word, we find that the chasm between assurance and security is not too broad at all. God's grace saves and God's grace enables His children to persevere, forming the bridge from security to assurance. This is comforting indeed!

PROPITIATION

Kevin T. Bauder

Like a traitor, scorning justice,
Head unbowed before God's Law,
Given glimpses of the Holy,
Tyranny was all I saw.

Soul infused with serpents' venom,
Purposing unholy war,
Hands devising clever mischief,
All of this was I, and more.

He, dispensing awful justice,
Haled me up before His throne,
Bound on me the grave indictment
Of commandments hewn in stone.

"Answer now," the judge demanded,
"Justify yourself to me.
Saints and angels wait your answer—
Enter your judicial plea."

I, exposed by blinding justice,
Naked in its righteous glare,
Stripped of every self-deception,
Stood with nothing to declare.

"Guilty!" uttered heaven's ruler.
"Guilty!" echoed hosts on high.
"Guilty!" charged my trembling conscience.
Guilty, and condemned to die.

Then the shouting storm grew soft, the
Shuddering of the earth grew still,
Blazing glory darkened, smoldered,
Waiting for the judge's will.

Crushed beneath the graven statutes,
Prostrate in the judgment hall,
Cringed I from impending judgment—
Dreadful fire about to fall.

Multitudes in glooming silence,
Wrath inscribed on every face—
Heard each one a small voice utter,
"I will take this sinner's place."

"Lay his guilt on my account, and
Let Thy righteous will be done.
May Thy Law be satisfied!" Thus
Pled for me the Judge's Son.

"Thou art My Beloved Son, Thou
Firstborn from eternity."
These words spake the Holy One, then
Turned His loving gaze toward me.

"Strip this sinner of his guilt, and
Grant My Son as He has prayed.
Lay on Him the Law's demand—now,
LET THE PRICE BE PAID."
Thirsty whips and thudding hammers,
Iron nails and angry thorns—
Darkness grows as guiltless suffers;
Stunned to blackness, Heaven mourns.

Like a Lamb, offered to justice,
Bloodied, broken by God's Law,
In His person, ever holy,
Guilt—my guilt—was all God saw.

　　　* * *

Stands the sacrifice complete, for
Justice has been satisfied.
Vengeance here is spent, exhausted,
Once the Lamb of God has died.

Now again the Mighty Savior
Lives enthroned as God the Son:
Goodness, justice, judgment, mercy
Reconcile in Him as one.

My whole duty is to trust, for
He alone can free the soul.
Rightly seeks He my submission;
Lovingly I yield, heart-whole.

Here I kneel in adoration,
Fear displaced by grateful trust,
In the Captain of Salvation—
Justifier, yes! and just.

FIVE

The Life of Prayer and Praise

e

HEART OF PRAYER

Kevin T. Bauder

*T*he night before He was crucified, Jesus spent an extended period teaching His disciples. Apparently He began His instruction while they were in the upper room, then continued to teach as they left the room and walked toward Gethsemane. Part of what He said centers upon the image of the vine and branches, reported in John 15:1-8. Specifically, in the context of this image, Jesus uttered the command to "abide in me."

Interpreters are about evenly divided on the significance of this command. Some understand abiding in Christ to refer to salvation; others take it to refer to some experience beyond salvation that Jesus wanted His disciples to enjoy. Of course, arguments can be advanced on both sides of this debate. I don't intend to go into all of them here. In my opinion, verse 3 is decisive: the disciples to whom Jesus addressed this command were already believers whose sins had been cleansed by His Word. They were already saved, and they were not in any danger of losing the salvation that they had received. To me, it seems necessary that "abiding in Christ" must refer to some experience subsequent to the reception of Jesus as Savior.

The point of the passage is not about getting saved. It is not even necessarily about growth. The passage is about fruitfulness. A branch (a believer) is able to bear fruit only if it is connected to the vine (Christ). However, not all branches that are connected to the vine will necessarily bear fruit. The branches that do not bear fruit will experience judgment (v. 6), which most likely refers to chastening and removal from service (compare this to 1 Cor 11:30).

The connection between the vine and the branches is essential, but unlike real grapevines, the branches on this vine have the capacity to make choices of their own. Those choices will greatly affect their fruitfulness. The main choice that they have to make is whether or not to abide in Christ.

Abiding in Christ is not a one-way activity. "Abide in me," says Jesus in John 15:4, "and I in you." Abiding in Christ implies some sort of reciprocal relationship. "Abiding" is a relationship of exchange and mutuality.

The nature of this relationship is clarified by the preceding context. In John 14:21 Jesus states that a person who loves Him will be loved by the Father and, indeed, by Jesus Himself. Jesus adds, "and I will manifest myself to Him," describing a relationship of reciprocal love in which Jesus somehow becomes apparent to the person who loves Him. But how?

That question seems to have puzzled the disciples as much as it puzzles us today. Speaking for the disciples, Judas (the *other* Judas, as John makes clear) asks, "How will you manifest yourself to us, and not to the world?" Jesus replies that someone who loves Him will keep His words, and the Father will respond with an answering love. More than that, Jesus and the Father will come to such a person and "make our abode with him" (John 14:23).

In other words, Jesus promises that He and His Father will take up residence or make a home with each person who truly loves Jesus and seeks to honor Him. The word for "abode" (residence, home) is the cognate noun for the verb that is translated "abide" in John 15. The abode of John 14:23 and the abiding of John 15:4 are almost certainly denoting the same thing. The divine side of this abiding is promised in 14:23; the human side is required in 15:4.

The abiding, then, is simply living together. To "abide in Christ" is to live together with Him. It is a matter of consciously and deliberately taking up residence with a Savior whom we love and who has taken up residence with us.

Living with another person always requires some adjustments. Collegians discover this when they are assigned their first roommates. Living together involves a process of getting used to one another, learning one another's likes and dislikes, and accommodating one another's habits and peculiarities. It necessitates an attitude of give-and-take. Roommates who will not make some concessions for the sake of harmoniously living together swiftly become nuisances to those around them.

This process is even more pronounced when a couple marries. A new bride and groom cannot possibly foresee all of the ways in which they are going to have to adjust to each other. Each carries a lifetime of habits, preferences, and family traditions, some of which will grate upon the other mate. Where will they squeeze the toothpaste tube? Which way will they hang the tissue on the roller? Which vegetables will they eat? The erstwhile bachelor may be unnerved to discover that he is no longer allowed to put away his clothes all over the floor. The new bride may be startled to learn that her husband considers cola and cheese curls to be a balanced meal.

How will the couple process such differences? One way would be for each to insist upon her or his rights. If each partner is determined to maintain all the old habits undisturbed, then the marriage is in deep trouble from the very beginning. In a truly loving relationship, however, the partners will not be nearly as interested in getting their own way as they are in pleasing the other, the beloved. For such a couple, learning to live together becomes an ongoing process of joyful surrenders in order to delight the other. In this atmosphere, mutual care flourishes. Incidentally, the process never ends: couples who have been married for decades can still be discovering anew what delights the other.

This, I think, is the image that Jesus has in mind when He commands, "Abide in me." This command assumes that He and His Father have made Their home with us. Now we must learn to live with Jesus. We must become aware of His presence in our lives. We will want to learn what displeases or disappoints Him so that we may avoid it. We will wish to discover what pleases and delights Him so that we may pursue it. As we abide in Christ, this pursuit becomes a lifelong calling. Abiding in Christ means communing with Him, recognizing His place in our lives, and shaping our lives around His presence.

This kind of "abiding" life is what assures us of answers to our prayers (John 15:7). These answers will be abundant, for if we are truly abiding in Christ we will be asking for the very things that He Himself wants us to have. We will be seeking only those things that would genuinely delight Him.

In fact, abiding in Jesus is really the heart of prayer. It is the foundation upon which an effective prayer life is built. In a certain sense, it is itself prayer, for what could be more fundamentally prayerful than communion with Christ Himself? While prayer certainly includes asking, good asking is the result of a life lived with an awareness of the presence of Christ. Abiding in Christ means knowing Him, adoring Him, honoring Him, and seeking to please and to delight Him in all that we do.

ADORATION

Kevin T. Bauder

*J*ohn R. Rice used to be fond of saying that "prayer is asking." In the strict and technical sense, he was correct. The English verb *pray* means *ask*. The biblical concept of prayer, however, is much broader. It includes several related practices or modes of prayer. What they all have in common is that they are addressed to God.

Even the New Testament terms for prayer reflect certain distinctions. The most common terms are *proseuche* (prayer) and *deesis* (supplication). The word *proseuche* is the generalized term for prayer. It refers more or less to scheduled prayer, the sort of prayer in which one might engage during daily devotions. The word *deesis*, however, is a term for desperation prayer. It refers to the kind of prayer that we offer when the need is urgent and the answer cannot wait. Paul repeatedly links these two, speaking of the "prayer and supplication" that he offers to God.

The broader term *proseuche*, which refers to regular, scheduled prayer, includes several modes of praying. It consists of all the things that we do in our regular prayer life. Confession, thanksgiving, petition, and intercession are all aspects of *proseuche*. So is adoration.

Adoration is worship. It is praise. It is the acknowledgement of the perfections of God and the reflection back to Him of our wonder at those perfections.

Adoration is not the same thing as thanksgiving. We give God thanks for His gifts. Implicit in thanksgiving is the assumption that we have received some good from the hand of God. Thanksgiving is, first, the recognition that the gift comes from God, and, second, the expression of gratitude over what God has given.

Where thanksgiving is about God's gifts and our gratitude, adoration is about God's person and our awe. We give thanks when we recognize what we have received from God. We express adoration when we recognize who God is.

Adoration is praise or admiration, and we can admire and praise things from which we do not personally benefit. In fact, we can even admire and praise some things that work against us. For example, on the basketball court we might lose a game because the opposing team has a wonderfully gifted player. We may not be particularly thankful for such a player at the moment he is knocking us out of the playoffs—but if he is really a great athlete, we will not be able to help admiring him.

In the same way, we could and should admire God even if He never did anything for us. He would still deserve to be adored, praised, and worshipped simply because of who He is. Adoration is about His worthiness, not about our wealth.

Of course, God _does_ do things for us. In fact, He showers us with undeserved kindness. When God does give us gifts, those gifts are also confirmations of His character. Therefore, we should never be content merely to thank God for what He does for us. His gifts should move us to thanksgiving, but they should also move us to praise. We should admire God as the Great Giver. But we would also be obligated to admire Him if He never gave us anything.

Nature sometimes evokes a sense of admiration in us. When we come suddenly upon a beautiful rose or a surging waterfall or a mountain vista, we are often moved to pause, direct our attention to the sight, and simply enjoy it. The beauty itself deserves such a response. If we knew of someone who could not be moved by such beauties, we would think that something was wrong with that person.

Our God is infinitely beautiful and majestic in His person. We sometimes find ourselves face to face with His grandeur. Such moments may catch us as we read the Word, as we sing the great hymns, as we hear the Scriptures expounded, or as we ponder God's character in our meditations. When those moments arrive, our hearts should be forced to pause, contemplate the Divine Beauty, and rejoice with powerful wonder and admiration.

God's mighty deeds reveal His character. They show Him to be a Creator, Sustainer, Judge, Deliverer, and Redeemer. His acts in history reveal His wonderful power, holiness, justice, compassion, and love. Those deeds are recorded for us in the narratives of Scripture, and by reading the stories we can in a certain sense relive them in our hearts and minds. When we behold the goodness of God in creation, the justice of God at Sinai, the faithfulness of God to David, and the astonishing love of God on the cross, our hearts *have* to be moved. How can we not marvel at such a God?

The Psalms are filled with ponderings upon God's character. The prophets gaze deeply into the divine nature. The Gospels show us the astonishing mystery of God made man. In their letters, the apostles reason both from and toward the character of God. Throughout the pages of His Book, God places Himself on display. He shows Himself and sets Himself forth, not so that we can engage in disinterested inspection, but so that we might adore Him.

Every part of Scripture sets God before us in His goodness and greatness, His beauty and majesty. Every page of the Book should lead us to see Him in His wonderful glory. We should not be able to read a chapter of the Bible without being moved to acknowledge His perfections and to reflect back to Him our sense of awe and admiration at who He is.

Adoration is not merely a useful adjunct to prayer. It is the very center of the prayer life. Unless we are motivated by a strong sense of adoration, the prayer life becomes grasping, selfish, and stunted.

Adoration is our first and highest calling. For this we were made. For this we were redeemed. Until our hearts find their rest, delight, and satisfaction in God, they will have no rest. We cannot glorify God in the world until we have glorified Him first in our hearts.

EMOTION IN HYMNODY

Kevin T. Bauder

O ne objection often raised against a certain kind of church music is that it is "too emotional." Those who raise this objection often add that the purpose of church music is to communicate doctrine. For evidence they cite Colossians 3:16, "teaching and admonishing one another in psalms and hymns and spiritual songs."

I am all in favor of doctrinal hymns. In fact, I agree that everything we sing should express right doctrine. In itself, however, strong doctrinal content does not rule out emotional expression.

I do not believe that music can be *too* emotional. This is *especially* true of doctrinal hymns. The regenerate heart irresistibly resonates with spiritual truth. The more profound the truth, the more sensitively it is expressed, and the more clear its relationship to the believer, the more deeply the pious heart will be moved. The ability to evoke and express this right response is what separates hymnody from prose.

What principles, then, should regulate the expression of emotion in church music? Two are especially relevant.

First, though good hymnody may *express* deep emotion, it is not *about* the emotion. Right emotion must be grounded in reality. When the focus shifts from the spiritual reality to the emotion itself, the emotion is no longer rightly grounded. The purpose of hymnody is to adore God, not to admire ourselves. By concentrating on our own emotions, we transform hymnody into a mode of self-assertion.

Second, good hymnody must attach the proper emotions to the realities that are being considered. We recognize intuitively that hymnody must not express emotions such as anger with God or hatred toward Him. We know that good hymns do not mock God. Simply avoiding these egregious errors, however, does not ensure that a hymn communicates ordinate affection.

This raises a problem. All of our words for emotions are rather vague. They cover a lot of territory. The word *fear*, for instance, describes the way that one person recoils from spiders, the way that another reacts to a precipice, and the way that someone else feels about failure. One person feels *awe* when gazing into a starry sky, while another is awed when cherishing a newborn child. A particular man experiences *love* for his wife, his parents, his children, a good football game, and a plate of spaghetti.

I have mentioned three emotional terms: *fear*, *awe*, and *love*. Each of these words is used to denote several different feelings. A person who is startled by a spider is not feeling the same emotion as the person who dreads the semester finals, though both will say that they are afraid. Someone who is awed beside Niagara Falls is not experiencing the same emotion as someone who is awed by holding his firstborn. The kind of love that is proper toward a faithful dog is anything but proper toward a faithful wife.

Each emotional word describes several different feelings. This fact carries enormous implications for Christian life and worship. We ought to feel and express a range of emotion toward God. We must fill our worship with joy, awe, fear, and love. Not just any awe, or fear, or joy, or love will do, however. We must learn the right fear of God, the right love, the right awe, the right joy.

A wife would have reason to feel upset if her husband showed her the same love that he might rightly demonstrate toward a basset hound. Dare we think that God does not have reason to be vexed if we offer Him the kind of love that a teenage girl might offer a rock star? We ought to rejoice in our God, but can a pious man joy in God in the same way that a drunkard rejoices in whisky?

Questions like these are especially relevant to our hymnody. Christian hymns both express and shape our emotions toward God. Wrong emotion (inordinate affection) in our hymns will devastate our spirituality and our worship. In some ways, mislabeled emotions are even more damaging than mistaken doctrines. Doctrines are public and discursive. We can easily examine and compare them. If someone believes a wrong doctrine, then we simply point him to the right one. To show him the truth is to convict him of error.

Emotions are not like that. They are inward, private, and irreducibly personal. We cannot examine another's emotions in the same direct way that we inspect his theology. Comparing and critiquing our emotions is a much more difficult task than comparing and critiquing our doctrines.

Suppose that two men say that they love their wives. One man's idea of love is shaped by Elizabeth Barrett Browning, while the other man's idea of love is shaped by Hugh Hefner. Leaving aside the question of which love (if either) is the proper love for a wife, what is clear is that these two men do not mean the same thing when they talk about loving their wives. At least one of them is not fulfilling the obligation to love his wife.

Therein lies the problem. Each man considers himself to be a loving husband. As long as he believes that he is fulfilling his duty as a husband, he will not change. He will not repent while he believes he is righteous. It is no help if the man insists that he is sincere and that his affection is genuine. If a man loves his wife like he loves his dog, then the sincerity and intensity of his love is precisely the problem. When a man assures his wife that he loves her more than he loves any other dog, it is no compliment. The only solution is for the man to stop loving with the wrong love and to begin loving with the right one.

Emotions are powerful things, and a misdirected emotion can do powerful damage. Perhaps this is why some people would like Christian music not to be emotional. That is surely a wrong reaction, however. Our hymns must be emotional, but they must not be about emotion. They must be emotional, but they must express the right emotions for the spiritual realities that move us.

DIMENSIONS OF THE SACRED

Kevin T. Bauder

O ne of the marks of the emerging churches is a certain kind of rejection of the distinction between the sacred and the secular. Of course, pious people have always insisted that none of life is secular, that all of life is (or ought to be) lived as worship to God. The pietistic approach is to extend the rubric *sacred* to all of life so that even life outside of church is regarded as sacred.

Exactly the opposite is happening in the emerging churches. They have reasoned that, if there is no distinction between sacred and secular, then the corporate worship of the church can and should include the ordinary activities of life. Virtually anything can be brought into worship.

This philosophy had been growing for some time before the emerging churches began to emerge. For several decades, American evangelicals and fundamentalists have displayed a tendency to bring everything but the kitchen sink into their public worship. The practice of the emerging churches simply brings this trend to its reasonable conclusion.

A good bit of confusion could be cleared up if we were to remember that the sacred has more than one dimension. In other words, the term *sacred* can refer to more than one thing. I am going to argue that we use the word in at least two major senses. For the sake of convenience, I shall designate these as the "inner" and "outer" dimensions of the sacred.

By the outer dimension I mean that dimension of the sacred that we encounter outside of the assembled church. This dimension of the sacred is an aspect of our everyday lives. It stands in contrast to the secular.

The notion of secularity comes from the Enlightenment. It involves the detachment of some aspect of life from divine interest and superintendence. To be secular means to live as if God has no interest in a particular area of life, as if He has nothing to say about it, as if that area is simply disconnected from whatever religious beliefs a person may hold.

I suspect that most church members are practicing secularists much of the time. They do not understand how God is interested in or glorified by their employment, their avocations, their amusements, or their domestic life. They restrict their religion to the confines of the church.

Biblical Christianity explicitly disavows secularism. For the biblical Christian, none of life is detached from God. None of it is outside of His interest or purview. For the Christian, even such a mundane thing as eating and drinking is to be done to the glory of God.

In this sense, biblical Christians see all of life as sacred. Everything is done with an awareness of God's glory and Christ's lordship. Every activity of life is performed as an act of worship, for whatever cannot be done to the glory of God has no place in the life of a believer.

To say that all of life is worship, however, is not to say that all of life takes the shape of explicitly religious activity. We worship God best in our lives by remembering that whatever we have is from Him, by receiving it with thanks, and by using it according to His purpose. A worker worships God, not so much by passing out tracts to co-workers, but by doing excellent work. An artist worships God, not only by painting religious art, but by depicting ordinary subjects as God sees them. A husband worships when he kisses his wife, not by thinking about God, but by thinking about *her*. In a flower garden, one worships God best by enjoying the beauty of the flowers, realizing that their beauty is a mere suggestion of the glory of their Creator.

For the biblical Christian, the whole world is sacred. The earth is bursting with worship, for everywhere is the potential to bring glory to God. This is the outer dimension of the sacred.

The inner dimension of the sacred involves the deliberate worship of the gathered people of God. When they gather to worship their Lord, they constitute a temple—indeed, a holy of holies. The congregation that assembles to worship God creates its own space, and that space is sacred. We are not free to bring into the temple all of the things that we enjoy in our daily lives.

The ancients had a way of expressing this exclusion. What was permitted in the temple was sacred. What was not permitted in the temple was to be kept outside, in front of (*pro*) the temple (*fanum*). For a thing to be "profane" meant, not that it was unclean or immoral, but that it was ordinary, common, or everyday. Such things had no place in the corporate worship of the temple, and the things of the temple were never to be treated as profane (ordinary or everyday).

For example, to take the Lord's name in vain means to treat it as an ordinary or common word. That is precisely to "profane" the name of God. Profanity is not about cursing God; it is about using His name (and hence, regarding His person) as a common, everyday thing.

We also become guilty of profanity when we introduce the ordinary or everyday activities of life into the worship of the temple. The local church is a temple, the final purpose of which is to engage corporately in the worship of God. Here, the worship is deliberate and it must be focused upon God's person and His mighty deeds. Any distraction from God, who alone is the center of worship, is a profanation.

For example, in everyday life, kissing his wife is a virtuous and moral thing for a husband to do. It may even be obligatory. Under the rubric of the outer dimension of the sacred, each man should kiss his wife to the glory of God. This kissing may and should be an act of worship to the One who created the woman, instituted marriage, and gave the couple to one another. In the public worship of the assembled church, however, we would not call upon a man to lead the congregation in a season of wife-kissing. To do so would be unfit, inappropriate, and perhaps mildly obscene (an obscene act is one that ought not to be viewed under the circumstances). It would be a distraction from the purpose of the gathering, inasmuch as most men have difficulty concentrating on other things while they are kissing their wives.

Which activities may be brought into the corporate worship of the assembled church? The short answer is this: we only know what pleases God in corporate worship when He Himself tells us what does. We may perform only those acts that He has told us to perform. When it comes to the worship of the church, we must look for biblical authorization for every element that we include. To do less is to profane the worship of our God.

The sacred has an outer dimension. That dimension comprises every act in ordinary life that may be performed to the glory of God. But the sacred also has an inner dimension. That dimension permits into our corporate worship only those elements that God has authorized.

SHALL WE KEEP SABBATH?

Kevin T. Bauder

*D*ispensationalists often dismiss the Fourth Commandment as an aspect of that Law from which Christians have been set free, reasoning that believers during the church age need not concern themselves with Sabbath observance. Even if they acknowledge that the other nine commandments ought to be observed today, these dispensationalists are quick to note that the Sabbath commandment is never repeated for church saints. For many, that argument is sufficient to settle the matter.

Exodus 20:8, however, must be understood in its context, and its context includes the overall story line of the Pentateuch. The Sabbath was not simply fabricated at Sinai. Rather, it was inaugurated as an aspect of creation week, and creation is when God first blessed and sanctified it (Gen 2:1-4). In the giving of the Law, God specifically linked Sabbath observance to the natural order of creation (Exod 20:9-10). Indeed, Israel had already been keeping Sabbath even before the Decalogue was revealed (Exod 16:26-30).

Most Sabbatarians (Sabbath-keepers) are of two sorts: strict or modified. Both sorts of Sabbatarians wish to maintain Sabbath as a day of worship and rest. In some instances, they are even willing to enact legislation to enforce rest during the Sabbath by requiring that businesses be closed.

Strict Sabbatarians understand that the Sabbath day is, properly, the seventh day—i.e., Saturday. They are committed to a strict observance of the Sabbath, and therefore they observe Saturday and not Sunday as a holy day. Strict Sabbatarians are sometimes overt legalists, such as Seventh Day Adventists, but other times they may trace themselves to a more evangelical tradition, such as Seventh Day Baptists.

Modified Sabbatarians see the Lord's Day—Sunday—as a replacement for the Sabbath day. While they vary in the rigor with which they observe the day, they still insist that it must be characterized by worship and rest. Sporting activities, commerce, and unnecessary labor are all proscribed.

The rigors of Sabbatarianism have given Sabbath observance an unappealing image, to say the least. The popular impression is that keeping Sabbath is boring, stultifying, restrictive, unproductive, and onerous. That impression is unfortunate, for it runs directly contrary to the teachings of the Lord Jesus Christ. He said that Sabbath was made for humanity, i.e., that it was made as a thing that is good for people (Mk 2:27).

What I would like to propose is a kind of "soft" Sabbatarianism. I ground this Sabbatarianism, not in the Sinai code, but in the created order. By understanding why God rested, we discover the meaning of Sabbath rest in general. Once we have done that, we find that Sabbath is not a burden but a delight.

Genesis 2:2-3 informs us that God rested on the seventh (Sabbath) day, and that He consequently blessed that day and set it apart. It would be puzzling indeed if being blessed and hallowed by God turned the day into oppressive drudgery! No, clearly God meant this day to be beneficial.

What could it possibly mean that God rested? In answering this question, we must avoid two errors. First, we must not suppose that God was tired and needed to refresh Himself after a hard week of creation. Certainly an omnipotent God could not be exhausted that easily—or at all! Second, we should not conclude that God became inactive, for the world could not survive an instant without His sustenance and Providence. God was active, sustaining His creation and upholding all things, yet somehow He rested. But how?

A human analogy may help to clarify the answer. Imagine the first hot day of spring, and imagine that your lawn needs care. You mow the grass, then mow a second time to make it look like a fairway at a golf course. You edge all the walks, trim all the shrubs, and bag all the clippings. You pull every dandelion and carefully manicure the flower beds. After several hours, you have completed your work. What is the next thing that you will do?

Nine out of ten people will get a cold drink, park a chair or lounge in the middle of the yard, sit down, and simply gaze upon what they have completed. They will enjoy the spectacle of the even green grass, the orderly shrubs, the sharply-edged walks, and the smartly-dressed flowers. They will congratulate themselves on a job well done. They will simply delight in what they have accomplished.

That, I think, is what God was doing on the seventh day. He was delighting in what He had made. He had just fashioned a perfect creation. Everything He made was very good. God had every right to congratulate Himself on the wonder of His work. He had every right to rejoice and take pleasure in it. That is how God rested.

Consequently, Sabbath rest is not primarily about avoiding exertion or remaining immobile. To be sure, when one has given six days to hard, physical labor, inactivity may come as a welcome respite. But what about the person who sits at a desk for five days out of the week? For both people, Sabbath rest is different from mere immobility.

Sabbath rest is about delighting in God the Giver and in His good gifts. This makes Sabbath activity a natural conjunct of the Lord's Day. Corporate worship fulfills a major purpose of both events as Christian people rejoice in their Savior and magnify Him.

Worship is not the only ordinate activity for Sabbath, however. In a "soft" Sabbatarianism, we may pursue any activity that leads to an occupation with God and His goodness, or that produces a sense of delight and gratitude for His good gifts. Such activities might include enjoying thoughtful conversation among friends, taking pleasure in the beauty of creation, delighting in good food, in family, and in one's spouse. There is warrant for the Sunday dinner (especially if it is prepared mostly on Saturday), Sunday visitors, Sunday naps, and sometimes even the Sunday drive.

We need such times. They refresh our bodies and restore our souls. Sabbath rest is a blessing from God, a good thing that God has instituted for our own wellbeing. While we will choose to forego activities that disturb our composure and distract our attention from God and His goodness, Sabbath rest is far from onerous. Sabbath is to our spirits what oxygen is to our bodies: we may try to live without it, but if we go too long, we will not be able to catch our breath.

PONDERING THE WORKS OF GOD

Sam Horn

*W*e begin to appreciate our relationship to others when we start to realize how they have invested themselves in our lives. This realization deepens our understanding of the nature and character of the one with whom we enjoy the relationship. That is how we grow in our relationships with other people. It is also how we grow in our relationship with God.

As we consider how God has worked on our behalf, we gain deeper understanding of who He is and what He is like. Repeatedly, the writers of Scripture call Old Testament Israel to remember and recount the works of God. Often, these exhortations occur in contexts that encourage God's people to place their confidence and trust in Him (Ps 40:4-5; 66:5; 78:7). Remembering His awesome works on their behalf was an important means of helping the Israelites place their confidence in Him rather than in themselves or in the false gods of the surrounding nations.

Like Israel, God's people today need to place their confidence in God alone. Consequently, like Israel, we need to reflect regularly on His awesome works. For many, God's works are distant memories rather than present realities. They are experienced vicariously or, at best, corporately. That is why the Scriptures call us to personal reflection on God's work in our own individual lives.

This process can be helped by questions like, "What has God done for you personally in the last seven days to show you that He is at work in your life? What prayer has He answered? How has He met a specific need?" These questions personalize our reflections by forcing us to ask, "How has God been at work in, around, and through me?" This kind of personal reflection upon God's work will produce several important spiritual benefits.

The first is confidence in the Word of God. God's works remind us of the reliability of His Word, for the two are linked. God has given His children specific promises in the Bible. As we reflect on God's gracious activity in our lives, we discover how He keeps His promises.

For example, God has promised to meet all our needs according to His riches in glory by Christ Jesus (Phil 4:19). And we do have needs. We often find ourselves articulating our desperate need for His provision in some area of our life. When God answers, we should discipline ourselves to remember His work of mercy in our lives. The regular practice of this discipline will remind and assure us that God keeps His Word. It will build our faith and reliance on God's Word in other areas of life.

We learn about God's constancy when He keeps His Word to meet our needs and when we experience His provision. That same constancy should remind us that God also keeps His Word in how He deals with our sins. This knowledge will further motivate us to avoid sin and to guard against spiritual carelessness and complacency.

Remembering God's work in our lives increases our confidence in His Word. It also stimulates us to obey God. Constantly reviewing God's gracious, personal intervention in our lives protects us from becoming complacent or passive in our relationship with God. A God who is distant and uninvolved will quickly fade from our daily consideration. We may remember Him at appropriate religious intervals or in times of need, but practically He becomes a non-factor in our daily lives. When God's acts constantly remind us of His intimate presence in our lives, however, then we are more likely to give Him proper consideration in every decision that we make.

This connection is illustrated in Psalm 106. In recounting Israel's history, the author reviews God's marvelous acts of intervention and provision for His people. Israel, however, did not attempt to understand God's works on her behalf nor did she remember His mercies. As a result, she soon forgot God's Word and walked in gross disobedience (Ps 106:7-12). Because she forgot the works of God, she failed to seek the counsel of God and soon found herself tempting God. The sad result of failing to remember God's works was that God granted the Israelites their sinful requests and sent leanness to their souls (Ps 106:13-15).

Contemplating God's work in our lives also produces a third benefit: our souls will be stirred to thankful worship and joyful adoration. As God personally acts for us, we will be moved to give our lives back to Him in consecrated worship. We often see this response by believers in the Bible. God's intervention or provision frequently provoked acts of sacrifice or worship. Abraham built altars and sacrificed to God after receiving the promise of a seed. After wrestling with God all night, Jacob named the location *Peniel* in memory of having seen God and experiencing His preservation. Samson's parents offered a sacrifice to thank God for His unexpected promise of a son. Hannah dedicated young Samuel to the Lord's service in thankfulness for God's gracious answer to her prayer.

So it is in our lives. As we contemplate God's past and present activity on our behalf, our hearts are stirred to worship. We marvel at His wisdom; we stand amazed at His power to deliver; we rejoice as undeserving recipients of His grace and goodness; we are astonished at the direct answers to our petitions; and we are left speechless at the unmistakable evidence of His love and personal interest in our mundane lives. No wonder we respond in worship.

Pondering the works of God gives us confidence in the Word of God, stimulates us to worship God, and leads us to a more committed walk with God. This list of benefits could be greatly expanded given time and space. One final benefit is worth noting, however. Simply put, pondering the works of God leads to greater confidence in the worthiness of God.

Each of God's works reflects one or more of His attributes. An act of deliverance, a need met, finances supplied, a desire granted, a specific prayer answered, an infirmity healed, a loved one saved: all are aspects of common Christian experience. Each one reflects multiple facets of God's attributes, such as His love, mercy, omniscience, omnipotence, holiness, justice, and omnipresence (to name just a few). Each testimony is a verbal reminder that God desires to show Himself strong on behalf of those whose heart is perfect toward Him (2 Chr 16:9). Every work of God in our lives reminds us of God's character and His utter reliability as a very present help in trouble (Ps 46:1). When we constantly review God's character through His works and we rely on His Word, then we will learn to trust in Him in future times of trouble.

The psalmist reminded Israel of her need to review the gracious works of God for each successive generation (Ps 78:4-6). The solemn and sacred duty of each generation was to ensure that those who came after them would remember God's gracious acts from the past. In so doing, each generation would be motivated to place their confidence (their hope) in God and to keep His commandments (Ps 78:7). Failure to remember and review these works of God, however, would lead future generations to forget God and to repeat the mistakes of those whose heart and spirit were not right and steadfast before God (Ps 78:8). Like Israel of old, we must maintain this discipline so that we might set our confidence in God with a right heart and spirit.

SIX

The Will of God

Anatomy of a Decision: Finding God's Will

Jonathan Pratt

*H*ow can we discern the Lord's will for our lives? Everyone must answer this question not only when facing major decisions of life (vocation, spouse, church home), but also the secondary questions about achieving important goals. Should I go to college? If so, where? How many children should we have? Should we rent or buy a home? Should I accept a job promotion? Would it be wise to consider a job offer from another company? Should I serve the Lord as a pastor in America or in a foreign country? Can I continue to care for my ailing spouse at home? At what age should I plan to retire? Many more questions could be listed.

Common wisdom from our culture suggests that the answers to life's decisions lie within. "Go with your gut." "Let your conscience be your guide." "If it feels good, do it." Perhaps a less narcissistic counselor might ask, "What makes the most sense financially?" "What will accomplish the greatest good for the greatest number of people?" "Which decision will create the best atmosphere for peace and unity?"

The followers of Christ know that by themselves these suggestions fail to consider the one and only source of true wisdom. The One who created all things and who providentially rules this creation has provided a Book in which He reveals His perfect will. This Word is a lamp for one's feet and a light for one's path (Ps 119:105). It is profitable for teaching, reproof, correction, and instruction in righteousness (2 Tim 3:16). It gives the ability to understand the fear of the Lord and to find the knowledge of God (Prov 2:1-5).

The Bible is the Christian's main resource when making decisions, but God has provided another means by which believers can receive guidance: the Holy Spirit. Just before He returned to the Father after His earthly ministry, Jesus promised His followers that the Spirit would be sent to give guidance (John 14:26; 15:26; 16:13). This promise is further substantiated by Paul when he speaks of the fact that believers are led by the Spirit in their Christian walk (Rom 8:14; Gal 5:18).

At this point, many believers experience anxiety. What if the Bible does not directly address the decision that one needs to make? How can I discern the Spirit's leading in regard to my specific question? While true believers desire to do their Father's will (John 10:27), they can also be tempted to follow fleshly desires that would entrap them and result in sinful actions (Jas 1:14-15). So the question remains for the believer, "How can I be sure that I am making the decision that best accords with the will of God?" I suggest four criteria for Christians to consider when seeking to determine the Lord's will.

The first criterion is conformity to Scripture. God will never lead a Christian to make a decision contrary to His revealed Word. Thus, entering a dating relationship with an unbeliever is against God's will (2 Cor 6:14). Drinking alcohol to the point of inebriation is unacceptable (Eph 5:18). Joining a church that has women in positions of spiritual authority over men violates Scripture (1 Tim 2:12). Regardless of the many scriptural justifications a person may consider in situations like these (e.g., I can witness to her if I date her; I can teach them what the Bible really means if I join with them), Christians must submit to what the Scriptures teach. Many foolish actions of Christians would be halted if the Bible were used as the guide it was intended to be.

The second criterion is wise counsel. Solomon reminds us that an abundance of counselors provides safety (Prov 11:14). And these are not to be just any counselors, but counselors who give *wise* instruction to seekers (Prov 1:2-7). Rarely will this type of wisdom for decision making come from one's peers, especially during one's youth. Rather, one should seek the advice of respected leaders from the past and present who personally know the individual and who can view the situation through biblically tinted lenses. The writer of Hebrews reminds us that we are to remember our leaders and to imitate their faith (Heb 13:7). One of the best ways for Christians to do this is to seek their counsel. After all, they "keep watch over your souls as those who will have to give an account" (Heb 13:17); they know you and desire your spiritual best.

This hunting for wise counsel does not stop when one reaches a particular age. In a recent decision to change ministries, I contacted several individuals: my father, a former pastor with whom I had served at a previous church, several close friends, my siblings, my brother-in-law who had formerly served alongside me in a local church, and my fellow pastors in the church I serve. I can gladly affirm that Solomon's words are very true indeed.

The third criterion is prayer. Unquestionably, God's people must seek Him in prayer when considering any decision. Whether we look to the example of Jesus in the Garden of Gethsemane (Mark 14:35-36) or Daniel and the prospect of facing lions (Dan 6:10) or Peter seeking guidance in ministry (Acts 10:9-16), the Bible is replete with examples of God's servants seeking His face for guidance. No Christian can ignore the biblical mandates for seeking God's guidance in prayer whether by direct command (Jas 1:5) or by implication (Phil 1:9-10).

In considering the importance of prayer in decision making, two cautions are in order. First, one might be tempted to think that prayer is an unnecessary or peripheral activity because of the mistaken assumption that prayer does not accomplish much (but see Jas 5:16b-18). Or it may be that people downplay prayer because they are afraid of how God might use prayer to impress upon them an answer they would rather not consider (e.g., Joshua and the Gibeonites—Josh 9). A second caution relates to using prayer to justify one's decisions rather than to seek the Lord's will. This type of justification might be shown when one excuses his foolish decision by saying, "I prayed about it," as if this mantra should take away everyone's objections. Even earnest prayer does not constitute permission to ignore the other three criteria mentioned here.

The fourth criterion is to find God's direction. One of the more subjective aspects of the decision making process is trying to understand how God might be leading through circumstances and human reason. We must be extremely careful not to misread this direction: once again, wise counselors add eyes to our viewing. Nevertheless, we ought to take account of the practical realities of the situation in which God has placed us. Drawing up a list of positives and negatives often helps us to step away from the emotion of a decision in order to think more objectively about what is actually at stake.

We may need to take small steps toward a particular decision in order to see if it is the one God has planned for us. This would appear to be the way that Jonathan approached his decision about attacking the Philistines in 1 Samuel 14:6: "And Jonathan said to the young man that bare his armour, Come, and let us go over unto the garrison of these uncircumcised: it may be that the LORD will work for us: for there is no restraint to the LORD to save by many or by few." Apparently, God would have made it obvious to Jonathan that he did not want him to attack, but in this case Jonathan's initiative was met with God's open door and a great victory was achieved.

In discerning God's will, God expects His children to use the minds, abilities, and information He has provided. This certainly appears to be the attitude James commends in 4:13-15. It involves paying attention to all four criteria.

These four criteria should provide ample help in securing God's direction in the decisions we face. Sometimes people make the error of thinking that finding God's will is like searching for hidden treasure—a delusive dream that God dangles out in front of us to antagonize and irritate us. Others try to use Gideon's approach, asking God to send them some divine sign of His direction. Still others use some bizarre dream or unusual circumstance as evidence of God's leading. Oddly, some employ the "God wouldn't want me to actually enjoy doing His will" philosophy that finds it obligatory to choose the most undesirable path. None of these approaches is wise or biblical. God reminds His children that they can trust unswervingly in His direction (Prov 3:5-6) and that He will give them the desires of their hearts (Ps 37:4). And, indeed, it is often by His deliberate design that the uncertainty of the decision making process causes us to depend more fully on God and not on ourselves.

Do you find yourself in the midst of a difficult decision? Follow God's revealed will, seek the counsel of godly advisors, pray for a spirit of wisdom and discernment, and think through the circumstances that God has arranged. May God give us joy in seeking and finding His will along this earthly path to glory.

GOD'S CALL TO SERVICE

Daniel R. Brown

N ext to salvation, the call of God to the gospel ministry is the single greatest qualifying mark for anyone who is a minister of the gospel. For this reason, ordination councils examine candidates in three separate areas: conversion, call to the ministry, and convictions on doctrine. The call of God is widely recognized as a priority by virtually every book on pastoral theology. These authors, crossing every spectrum of theological position, devote anywhere from a section to an entire chapter to the subject. Most churches usually ask a potential pastoral candidate to give an account of his call to the ministry.

Even after this emphasis in both our literature and our practice, the call of God has fallen upon hard times. My experience in ordination councils, as well as discussions with pastors, teachers, and students, indicates that a great deal of confusion and doubt surrounds the discussion of God's call to the ministry.

Several causes explain this lack of clarity about God's call to the ministry. First, authors tend to describe the call in their own terms. Consequently, variety abounds in how the call is defined and described. Second, the call of God is sometimes confused with a subjective, existential experience equivalent to someone saying, "God spoke to me." Third, some deny that God has an individual will for each believer. Since the notion of a call assumes both that God does have such a will and that it can be known, those people will necessarily reject the suggestion that God calls some to the ministry.

A word needs to be said about what the call of God is not. It is not a special visitation of God via a dream or vision. It is not a matter of opening up the right fortune cookie or seeing an apparition of Christ. It is not even a great conviction of the need for ministry.

Discerning the call of God involves a subjective aspect, just as understanding the individual will of God involves some subjectivity. We are rightly hesitant to give credence to subjective, unconfirmed speculations. We want believers to be grounded in the objective Word of God. Yet we do understand that there is a subjective aspect to our Christian life. For example, the Spirit testifies with our spirit that we are the children of God (Rom 8:16). Assurance of salvation involves an internal, subjective factor in addition to knowing and claiming the explicit, objective promises of Scripture.

God's call to the ministry includes two aspects. First, the call will include an overwhelming desire, and specifically a desire to preach. Two different Greek words are translated as *desire* in 1 Timothy 3:1: "If a man desire the office of a bishop, he desireth a good work." The first word (*oregetai*) means "to stretch oneself out in order to touch or to grasp something" (Abbott). It carries the idea of the runner that stretches for the finish line, desiring victory. This involves a desire or aspiration for the office. The second word that Paul uses (*epithumei*) is often found with a negative sense in the New Testament. This word is typically translated as "lust" when the object of the desire is improper. The root idea of the term means a "burning upon" or a "desiring with passion." In 1 Timothy 3:1, the sense is positive, but the strength of the term remains: "he desires (lusts for or covets) a good thing." The desire is not a whim or a passing fancy, but a passion that changes the course of one's life.

The second aspect of the call of God will be an inescapable conviction based upon the Word of God. The Scripture will grip a man's heart and, when coupled with a passion for the ministry,

will never release him. As this is an individual aspect of how
God leads to His call, no two preachers will have the exact same
experience or testimony. One pastor of my acquaintance has
described the call of God as a burden that does not go away.
In *Lectures to My Students,* Spurgeon discusses the call of God
by suggesting that if a man can be satisfied in any other line of
work, he should leave the ministry alone.

The call of God typically accompanies several other facets of
a man's life. First, he will express a desire to prepare for ministry.
Baptists have never set a minimum standard of education to
enter the ministry, but they certainly have not exalted ignorance
in the pulpit. Generally speaking, a call to preach is a call to
prepare. Second, a man will possess the ability to preach and
teach, at least in a rudimentary way. Handling the Word is
foundational to the task of the preacher. God's calling is also
His enablement. God does not call someone unable to perform
the task. Third, if called, a man should evidence some measure
of success in ministry. Others will recognize and agree that
God's hand is working in his life.

The call of God does not happen in a vacuum. Christ, in His
active role of church headship (Eph 1:22-23), calls and gives men
to the ministry of the church (Eph 4:11). In doing this, Christ
works in both the life of the minister and the life of the local
church. The Holy Spirit directs the call (Acts 13:2-3; 20:28) as the
active functionary in the life of both the minister and the local
church. Finally, the local church verifies the call (Acts 13:2-3).

The church has a special role in protecting the ministry from
unqualified and uncalled men. At minimum, the church should
agree with a man's call and qualifications prior to authorizing
his ministry. No man should enter ministry apart from the
blessing and cooperation of his church.

The call of God changes a man's direction and focus. The qualifications are high (1 Tim 3:1-7) and the commitment to gospel ministry dominates the direction of both the man and his family. The blessings of being a useful vessel for the Master are beyond measure. Thus the man of God can say with Paul, "He counted me faithful, putting me into the ministry" (1 Tim 1:12).

SEVEN

Testing and Temptation

e

WHY ME, LORD?

Jeff Straub

*I*t has been called *the problem of pain*. It has been addressed as *why bad things happen to good people*. It is used as an apologetic problem to discredit the truth claims of Christianity. Whatever form it takes, the problem of personal suffering is one of the most difficult challenges with which believers grapple. It strikes close to home.

Suffering provokes many questions. Why do people suffer? More specifically, why do I suffer? What did I do to deserve such pain? Is God angry with me? Is He punishing me or is He simply vindictive?

Questioning can easily lead to doubt and bitterness. We think that God must not care because of what He is allowing to happen to us. Our suffering is almost always worse than we think we deserve.

When Christians are confronted with this problem, how should they respond? What can be said when trying to console someone experiencing deep grief due to heavy suffering? Is there any real comfort for them?

More than twenty years ago, my wife and I had to struggle with these very questions. Our third child was born ten weeks prematurely. As we left the hospital, the doctors told us that our son would probably experience some form of a disability as he grew older. Specifically, we were told that he had a small inter-cranial bleed that would cause unknown problems as he developed.

By our son's first birthday, we could tell that he would not progress like our other two children. He could not roll over or sit up. By age two, he still could not walk or even crawl. At age three, he was given an electric wheelchair, and one has been part of his life ever since. He requires significant care to meet even his basic personal needs.

What did our son do to deserve this? What did we? His life is difficult and many would say that he lives a life of suffering.

Not even the Lord's disciples were immune to the concerns caused by suffering. In John 9, they questioned Jesus about this very issue. They saw a blind man. As far as they were concerned, blindness was obviously a result of sin. God must be punishing somebody—the man himself, or perhaps his parents.

To be sure, sin is the underlying cause of all human suffering. God warned Adam and Eve of dire consequences if they failed to obey His command in the Garden (Gen 2:16-17). Nevertheless, they broke God's law and suffering entered into the world. By man came sin and with sin came death. Even the death of Jesus Christ, the Son of God, was the result of human sin.

Some suffering is directly tied to individual sin. For example, in Acts 5 Ananias and Sapphira lied to the Holy Spirit and to the church at Jerusalem. Their duplicity resulted in their premature death (Acts 5:1-11). Similarly, Paul warned the believers at Corinth that failure to discern the Lord's body by taking the Lord's Supper "unworthily" had resulted in some of them being sick or even dying (1 Cor 11:30).

All suffering stems ultimately from sin, and some suffering is directly traceable to our own sins. That does not mean, however, that all suffering stems immediately from personal sin. We must not assume that if we (or our loved ones) are suffering, then we must have sinned.

God does not punish our children to even the score with us as parents. A child may suffer for the consequences of a parent's action—if I rob a bank and go to jail, my child may grow up without a father in the home—but that is not punishment for sin as far as my child is concerned. Innocent people are experiencing the consequences of others' actions but they are not being punished. The pain may be as severe, but we must not falsely charge God for an attitude He does not possess.

Children learn early that actions have consequences. If a girl does something "cute," her parents may laugh. If she does something "naughty," she will get scolded. God very clearly distinguished between the consequences for sin which may be passed on through several generations (Exod 20:5) and the punishment for sin which each individual bears alone (Deut 24:16): "The wickedness of the wicked shall be upon him[self]" (Ezek 18:20).

My child did nothing to cause his disability. He could have done nothing to prevent it. From a human perspective, his suffering is merely an accident, a fluke, a random chance event for which he must bear the life-long consequences. Yet the truth is greater than this.

Did God cause the disability? Could He have prevented it but chose to allow it anyway? If so, then why? It seems like a large burden for my son to bear—to be bound to a wheelchair for his entire life. Could he not rightly ask, "Why me, Lord?"

Christians encounter some questions that God simply does not answer. God's ways are not our ways (Isa 55:8) and He does what He does for His own purpose and glory. He "worketh all things after the counsel of his own will: that we should be to the praise of his glory, who first trusted in Christ" (Eph 1:11, 12). God wants to bring glory to Himself and He uses us to do this. He glorifies Himself in and through our lives. By allowing us a limited amount of suffering (Paul calls it a "light momentary affliction" [2 Cor 4:17]), God enables us to glorify Him by providing sufficient grace to bear the burden. Other people perceive God's grace in our lives and are transformed when they see that we face suffering, not with bitterness, but with God-given grace (2 Cor 12:9-10). God's power is perfected in our weakness.

One of the most frequently quoted verses for one Christian to offer as comfort to another is Romans 8:28, "And we know that all things work together for good to them that love God, to them who are the called according to his purpose." Paul says something similar in Philippians 1:6, "Being confident of this very thing, that he which hath begun a good work in you will perform it until the day of Jesus Christ." Twice Paul speaks of the "good" God is doing in our lives, despite the "bad things" that may be happening to us. But how can we be sure that the things that are happening to us are ultimately good?

We must learn to distinguish what happens *to us* from what happens *in us*. God is doing a work of grace *in* our hearts. Consequently, He may allow us to experience affliction that may affect our temporal circumstances but will not alter our ultimate destiny. Our eternal hope cannot be shaken by temporal trials. God has guaranteed our destiny and, though the journey may be difficult, the outcome is secure.

We can also have confidence that whatever God allows to be done to us will ultimately produce good—real, genuine good. How can we be sure of this? One obvious answer would be simply to say that the Bible says it and that settles it. The Apostle Paul insists that "all things work together for good."

In this case, however, we may be able to make even a stronger argument for affirming that God brings good out of suffering. We might ask how Paul himself could be so sure of this truth. The answer is that he grounds his observation in the character of God. Things that God is doing are good because God Himself is good. Since He is good (Ps 100:5), all that He does is good. Consequently, Paul can affirm the inherent goodness of God's work in our lives because the God who oversees our circumstances is Himself good.

Paul asserts much the same thing in Philippians 2:13, where he says that God works in us "to will and to do of his good pleasure." God is at work in my life, and His work is a good work. God is no mere bystander, passively looking on and wishing things had turned out otherwise. No, the Bible affirms that God is sovereign over the affairs of human life. In Ephesians 1:11, Paul argues that God is the one who "worketh all things after the counsel of his own will." The "all things" must be understood to be both positive and negative things in our life. In this assertion, Paul echoes the words of the psalmist who reminds his readers that God as Creator owns "His sheep" and cares for them (Ps 100:3).

God is sovereign over the affairs of life. These texts speak of God's active participation in what is happening. God permits things to happen in a certain way, and whatever way He permits them to happen is ultimately good.

We can and should take great comfort in the fact that God controls His universe. Things do not just happen in His world. He actively sustains it and controls it and orchestrates it so that the outcome He desires will prevail. The goal of His plan is good, and His children, as objects of His good pleasure, participate in that goal by becoming the recipients of God's good work.

What do these observations mean to Christians who suffer? First, they mean that God is not passive about our suffering. While He is not necessarily the active cause of all suffering, He is the one who permits it, just as He permitted the testing of Job (Job 1). Second, suffering has a purpose for believers. It is not just random bad luck. Because we know that God is in control of the events of life, we can take comfort even when we fail to comprehend all of the reasons behind our suffering. God is good and His decree will prevail. Finally, even when we cannot see where our suffering will take us, we can be sure that the goal is a good one. God is good, and His work is good, so the goal of that work must also be good—both for God and for us.

Suffering is never a pleasant experience. The pain can be severe. In the light of eternity, however, our temporal suffering is very brief. My son may be in a wheelchair now, but he has eternity to enjoy the use of his legs. Meanwhile, he can learn to love and to trust God from that chair. He can also learn to see the good hand of God working through the chair. As his parents, we too must see the good hand of God in all He does.

Bitterness and anger will not help my son. It will not solve my problem or alleviate any of the suffering. His suffering does not need to separate me from God. Instead, it can be used to draw me to God as I learn to trust in His will. I simply need to trust His Word. Since it says that "all things work together for good," then I must believe God and trust Him, even without knowing precisely how this happens. He who began a *good* work will finish it.

PSALM 121

Translated by Roy Beacham

I lift my eyes again unto the hills.
From where will my help come?
My source of help is the LORD, who made heaven and earth.
He will not allow your foot to stumble.
He who keeps you will not slumber;
Behold, he who keeps Israel will never slumber and never sleep.
The LORD is your keeper.
The LORD is your shade on your right hand;
The sun will not strike you by day or the moon by night.
The LORD will keep you from all evil.
He will keep your soul.
The LORD will keep your going and your coming
From now even to eternity.

MY KEEPER

Roy Beacham

I stand transfixed in anguish-riven fright
And view such heights as terrorize my soul;
My eye sees only shadow's waxing night,
While primal fears like earthen tremors roll.

I fain would look away, but cannot seem
To break the horrid spell that on me cast
This awful phantom; caught as in a dream
That wonders long if there be help at last.

Sure help there be! Though terror's echo sway,
The still small voice of One I finally hear.
He whispers sweet, "I am the LORD, your stay,
Look unto me, who fashioned that you fear."

This LORD, His hand is sovereign over all;
The smallest step is His to give or take.
He misses not the slightest beck or call;
In throes of darkness ever He's awake.

My Keeper, He; I know no better aid.
Where lies my weakest fault, just there He stands.
No burning flame shall ever breach His shade,
And phantom light is naught within His hands.

There is no evil come but meets His good,
This Keeper ne'er my soul will cast away;
My steps, each one, but tread the path they should,
Sore shades of earth, and then eternal day!

And so my feeble eyes, they turn at last;
No longer shadowed heights and terrors' pall,
But higher look; and on my Keeper fast
My gaze now fixed: my God, my peace, my all.

LETTERS TO A SOUL OVERTAKEN IN A FAULT

Kevin T. Bauder

One

Dear Soul,

You are fallen in sin. This we both know. You admit it. You are taking pleasure in things that are an offense to God. The fact that you can do this is no small distress to your brothers and sisters.

This sin of yours has been going on for a long time. At first it was secret while you still felt shame. Now it is open. It is not a simple matter of momentary weakness. Your sin has become a settled part of your life.

You admit that this thing is wrong, but you are not prepared to abandon it. Quite the opposite. You claim that this thing has become something that you very much desire. Indeed, you now say that you have come to love it. You claim that you cannot alter your affections at will, and you have begun to infer that loving your sin cannot be all that wrong. Consequently, even though you claim to be a child of God, your heart belongs at least partly to something that God hates.

You are asking me (and others) simply to accept the present state of affairs. I am writing to respond, but my response is not going to be as straightforward as giving a *yes* or a *no*. I am not interested in simply moralizing. You do not need moral preachments right now. They will not help you. What you need is to understand why your sin grips you so tightly, why you love it, and what can be done to change this situation.

We know that your sin is one in which you have indulged over a process of years, and your attachment to it has been cultivated over that entire time. Is it not true, however, that your feelings were already changing before you overtly yielded to the temptation? You did not simply wake up one morning and determine to spend the next several years of your life in sin. That is not how such things begin.

My guess is that for a long time before you yielded, you sensed a lack in your life. Some area seemed unaddressed or unfulfilled by your walk with God. You began to question God's goodness in that area. You began to wonder whether God really knew or even cared whether you experienced this lack. Over time, your affection for God was slowly eroded and you attempted to find your fulfillment in other things. None of those distractions, however, could take the place that only God can fill.

Is that not why this sin seemed so attractive when the possibility presented itself? You did not start out looking for sins to commit. The sin was a by-product of the attempt to find something that was missing in your life—something that you felt that you needed rather badly, even if you could not have said just what it was or how it would have made a difference.

The need that you felt was almost certainly a legitimate, God-given yearning. Even Satan cannot make up any new desires. He has to work with the ones that God has already given us. What he can do, however—and this is the essence of all temptation—is to induce us to meet a legitimate need or to fulfill a legitimate desire in an illegitimate way. In this way he disorders our feelings so that we begin to love the wrong things, or to love the right things in the wrong proportions, or to love them in the wrong way.

God gave you desires that could rightly be fulfilled only in certain ways. When those ways were not available, you entertained the possibility of directing your desires in ways that God has not permitted. Ultimately, you sought to fulfill them in ways that God had forbidden—through sin. These were the first steps in what theologians call "inordinate affection," or disordered desire.

Once you had made the decision to engage in the sin, another dynamic came into play. Do you remember what Jesus says about storing up treasure in heaven? He gives a reason, namely, "where your treasure is, there will your heart be also" (Luke 12:34). In other words, the things in which we invest are the things that we come to love. That is why it is so very important to be sure that we are investing in the right things.

Investments are not always merely financial. You have indulged in this sin for years. That means that you have made a major investment of time and energy. Your heart has followed your investment. No wonder. This is exactly what Jesus said would happen.

So we have seen two reasons for your attachment to your sin. The first is misdirected affection. The second is personal investment. Beyond these is a third reason.

We never define ourselves by ourselves. We always find our identity—we discover who we are—by our relationship to something outside of ourselves. We need certain fixed points in our lives to tell us who we are.

People try to find their identity in all sorts of things. Very often, men identify themselves by what they do or what they own. They define themselves by their careers and their possessions. A man's job becomes part of who he is. His car becomes an extension of his persona. Even his favorite football team can become part of his identity.

Women may do the same thing, but they are more likely to define themselves in relation to other people A woman often understands herself as the wife of a particular man or the mother of particular children. Relationships are very important (they are to men, too, but usually in a slightly different way).

The thing that constitutes our primary identity becomes who we are, at least in our self-understanding. Once we become so attached to a thing that we define ourselves by it, we have to protect that thing. Like Gollum's One Ring, it becomes our "Precious." If it dies, then we die.

There is a progress to sin, and these three considerations explain why some sins are so hard to give up. We begin by directing our desires toward an illicit object. Then we invest in that object and our heart becomes attached to it. Ultimately, it becomes so much a part of us that it constitutes our identity. To give it up feels just like dying. It seems as if we are killing a piece of ourselves.

I think that these considerations explain what you mean when you say that you love your sin. There is a terrifying risk in letting it go. You risk the fulfillment of God-given desires—after all, can you be sure that God will provide a righteous way for those desires to be met? You risk years' worth of investment (indeed, you are resigning yourself to its loss). Most of all, you risk losing track of yourself, of no longer knowing who you are. Does it not feel rather like killing part of yourself?

But here's the thing: God did not design men to find their identity in their work or their toys. God did not design women to find their identity in their relationships. God designed and intended us to find our identity in Him. He made us to know Him, to enjoy Him, and to love Him (Deut 6:4-5).

The thing by which we identify ourselves is our god. To treat it as the goal of our life—to sacrifice good and right things for it—is to assign ultimate value to it. This ascription of ultimate value is what we call *worship*. Whenever we make a thing an end in itself, we are worshipping it. To love a thing for its own sake is exactly to make it our god. It is to become an idolater.

That is why I think it is so wrong for you to go on loving your sin. Since the sin is clearly not God's will for your life, then you cannot be loving it for God's sake. Consequently, you must be loving it for its own sake, as if devotion to it could bring you genuine satisfaction. This love is idolatrous and, as long as you love your sin in this way, it is your god.

In terms of culpability, it really does not matter whether you are capable of willing a change in your emotions. When people feel the wrong things, we hold them to be disordered and even twisted. If a person hates what is beautiful and loves what is ugly, then that person is defective. Something is wrong with the individual who prefers garbage dumps and mud slides to roses and sunsets.

In extreme forms, disordered loves can even lead to perversions. Some people are drawn toward sexual love of children, animals, or members of their same sex. They may object that their feelings are not under the direct control of their wills, but we do not excuse them. In at least some cases we even pass laws against the expression of those feelings. A person who experiences such love must recognize it as a defect and must learn not to express it or even to entertain it.

In the end, all disordered loves lead to slavery. The idols always promise what they cannot deliver. If we cling to them, we shall find ourselves shattered and embittered. What we need is someone who can break our bondage and free us from the tyranny of our idols. We need a savior.

That is what Jesus Christ is to us. The gospel is not merely the message that Christ saves us from the penalty of sins. The gospel is the power of God that crushes the idols in our hearts and frees us from their cruel oppression. The gospel restores us to a right relationship in which we are given the ability to love God for Himself, as the ultimate good and goal of our lives.

Loving God gives us true freedom. Not only does it deliver us from the brutality of our idols, but it gives us the power to do what we could never otherwise accomplish. By loving God we rise above ourselves and above all petty loves. Rather than loving things for themselves or for the fulfillment that they seem to offer, we can begin to love them rightly for the sake of God.

Let me put it this way. If my wife has to love me for my own merits, then I am sunk. I know my own failings too well. If, however, she loves me for the sake of God, then I can feel truly safe in her love, for the God whom she loves will never fail. For my part, I can begin to try to love her in the impossible ways that Scripture requires: as Christ loved the church, for example, or as I love my own body. We will not only learn to love each other, but our love will be more properly proportioned and more of the right kind than it could ever otherwise have been. It will be an ordinate love, for it will be conditioned and defined by God's own love.

Under my love for God, there is a certain love that is right for me to show to my wife. There is another love that is right to show to my daughter, and yet another that is right for my son. There is a right kind of love for me to show toward material objects, natural beauty, and physical pleasures. There is even a right kind of love for me to feel toward you. In none of those loves will I ever have the problem that I love too much; indeed, I have never loved enough. But I must cultivate the right kind of love.

The question is not how much, but how to love these people and things. If I love them as they ought to be loved, then all of them can bring glory to God. To love them rightly means to love them for God's sake, as He Himself loves them.

Here we encounter a curious thing. When we love a thing for God's sake rather than as an end in itself, our love becomes expansive. We actually enjoy a thing more when our motivation is not simply to enjoy the thing in itself. In fact, the enjoyment of the thing may lead us into new and unforeseen loves, all under God and devoted to His glory.

When we love a thing for its own sake, however, our love atrophies. It becomes obsessive. When we give ourselves to a sinful love, we leave other loves behind. Our wrong love demands more and more from us, and it leaves us with less and less. In the end, even the thing itself begins to gall us, but we discover that we cannot let it go. Rather than opening new windows of joy, an inordinate love leads to deepening levels of misery.

Is this not the case? Since you gave yourself to a sinful love, do you not detect this pattern? You give yourself to your sin, but it cannot satisfy you. Have you not found that it demands more and more of your attention? That it distracts you from other pleasures? That it leaves you jaded and glutted while it demands more and more of your attention?

So now, here you are, left with torn and mixed affections. Granted, these are not directly under your voluntary control. That is not an excuse for feeling the wrong things, however. It is simply a statement of the problem.

These feelings can be changed. You did not get into them in a day or a week, and you will not get out of them in a day or a week. But they can be changed.

Fundamentally, what you need is to allow the gospel to re-orient you so that you come to understand who you are in Christ Jesus. You need to find your identity in your relationship with God. You need to learn to love Him with a love that answers to His love for you. As you do that, and as you are faithful to your duties, God will eventually transform your affections so that you love what He loves, as He loves it.

Above all, do not despair! Your heart is not beyond God's power to restore. In fact, if you will recognize what needs to change, and if you will devote yourself to learning to love the right things (God first, then other things for God's sake), then your life can be more satisfying than you have ever found it.

For you, this feels like a terrible risk. You are opening yourself up to hurt. You are surrendering a years-long investment. You are even sacrificing a large part of who you are, or at least who you think you are. What God is asking you to do will feel like dying. But God specializes in bringing life out of death, does He not?

Two

Dear Soul,

Since my last letter, you seem to have made no change. If anything, you are more entrenched in the idea that, since you cannot directly control what you love, God does not hold you accountable for it. As a brother, I wish that I might help you to see and understand what is at stake in the decisions that you are making.

More than anything else, God wants us to admire Him. In a human, that desire would be vain, and the reason is obvious. We are finite and created beings, and all of our best qualities are given to us as free gifts. The proper stewardship of our gifts is to direct the praise to the Giver. God, however, is infinite and uncreated. He is self-existent. Whatever He is, He is from

Himself alone. No one has ever given Him anything that He did not already have. He cannot ever owe anything to anyone. What He is passes description. He is simply the most fascinating, majestic, intricate, profound, and beautiful Being who ever has been or ever could be.

Have you ever seen a particularly spectacular sunset or an especially gorgeous flower garden? Did you not wish that you had a companion to share the view? Don't you find that the enjoyment of beauty increases when that enjoyment is shared with someone else? Nothing is more distinctively human than to want to share the best experiences. For that reason, God is not vain when He puts Himself on display and asks us to admire Him. Quite the contrary: because He is so magnificent, the most generous thing that He can do is to offer us Himself.

We were made to admire God. That is another way of saying that we were made to enjoy Him, to find pleasure in Him. We are created to need Him, and to need to exalt Him. In other words, we are created to worship the true and living God.

Granted, worshipping God is often seen as our chief duty, but it is more like our chief delight. We can enjoy no greater pleasure than God, for there is no glory—no beauty or nobility, no baffling intricacy or majestic simplicity—greater than the glory we encounter in God Himself. We are made to find our ultimate satisfaction in Him, because only He is ultimately satisfying.

My description might lead you to believe that our relationship to God is fundamentally one of distant appreciation, i.e., that we are to admire Him much as we might direct our awe toward a natural wonder like the Grand Canyon or Niagara Falls. Indeed, admiration and awe are certainly part of our relationship with God, but they are not the heart of the matter. Rather, God asks something else of us before we offer Him our adoration.

Most importantly, God asks us to trust Him. By this I do not mean simply that we must trust Him for salvation. If sin had never entered the world, if there were no condemnation or need for redemption, and if Adam had never eaten of the tree, nevertheless our fundamental relationship with God would still be one of trust. He created us to depend upon Him, and the life to which He invites us is a life of faith.

For the life of faith to make sense, you must remember who God is. He is infinitely loving and good, which means that He desires what is best for you. God will never wish for something that is ultimately bad for you. He desires your wellbeing so much that He gave His Son in sacrifice to redeem you to Himself (Rom 8:32). If He loves you enough to provide salvation, then He loves you enough to provide anything that could be for your ultimate good.

God is also infinite in knowledge and wisdom, which implies that He knows what is best for you. Not only does He know everything that is, was, or will be, He also knows everything that might have been. He knows the infinite variety of possible worlds in all their permutations. God knows exactly what is good for you—and what is better, and what is best.

Not only does God wish what is best for you and know what is best for you, but He also can do what is best for you. He is infinite in His power and sovereignty. He rules over His world, and nothing occurs without His permission. Sometimes He acts directly and sometimes He acts through secondary causes, but always He achieves what He sets out to do. He even takes the evil things that people plan and uses their wicked deeds in accomplishing His purpose.

God wants what is best for you. He knows what is best for you. He can do what is best for you. What He asks of you is that you trust Him for what is best.

That trust begins with a recognition that God's laws—the "thou shalts" and "thou shalt nots"—are not merely arbitrary rules, much less oppressive regulations. They are without exception designed for our good. When God requires something of us, it is because He knows that thing to be necessary. If He forbids something, it is because He knows it to be hurtful.

We are pitifully small. Our foresight is so limited that we cannot see a single minute into the future. We do not know the outcome of our circumstances and we cannot see where our choices will lead. God, however, knows and understands all these things. He invites us to trust Him in every detail of life.

The problem is that God does not usually work directly and miraculously. He typically employs secondary causes, and He uses them skillfully to affect our lives in amazingly intricate ways. A single event may represent a nexus of directions that impinge upon hundreds or even millions of eventual outcomes, yet each is under the oversight of the sovereign God.

Because God generally works through secondary causes, we rarely see His hand directly. If we are inattentive or forgetful, we begin to perceive the events of our lives as the result of circumstances. Then we begin to believe that we can manipulate these circumstances to a far greater degree than we actually can. We begin to suppose that we can choose the outcomes that we desire, and we assume that we can engineer our circumstances to achieve those outcomes. In short, we come to think that we ourselves control the destiny of our lives. We rely upon ourselves, assisted by a certain measure of luck (which is the term that we use for the alignment of circumstances that goes beyond our control). Rather than trusting God, we begin to trust ourselves and the natural order of events.

The problem with this approach is that neither self-reliance nor good fortune can lead us to genuine happiness or satisfaction. We are made to glorify God. Our souls are contoured for communion with Him. When we try to find our happiness in any finite thing—that is, when we worship an idol—we doom ourselves to ultimate frustration. No idol can bear the weight of a human soul. All idolatries are an exercise in futility. We may as well try to drink the wind or feed upon ashes.

Consequently, God in His mercy will occasionally place us under circumstances that are utterly beyond our control. Such circumstances are designed to remind us that we are neither the masters of our fate nor the captains of our souls. At such moments, God wishes us to remember that He alone is perfectly faithful and true. He wishes us to turn to Him and to cast ourselves upon Him in renewed trust.

As long as we are careless, distracted, and self-reliant, only the unpleasant circumstances seem to get our attention. In order to remind us of our dependence, God must allow affliction to enter our lives. Affliction takes different forms, from physical illness to bereavement to poverty to fractured relationships. These hardships are not sent by a vindictive and punitive Judge, but rather by a loving Father who wishes the best for His children. He knows that when we neglect to worship and fail to trust Him, we are overlooking the very things that would bring us the greatest happiness.

We find ourselves afflicted when our life lacks some good thing. If the deficiency is severe enough, then we experience it as a deprivation or need. If it involves the loss of something that we once enjoyed or expected to enjoy, then we also experience grief. At that moment, we must make a choice. Either we will trust God to provide a legitimate way of gaining the missing good (which means committing ourselves to living without it during the interim), or else we will seek to acquire the good through illicit means. In the first case, we are using our need as a way of glorifying God, recognizing that He Himself is the chief good. In the second case, we are choosing to sacrifice God in order to gain the missing good, which means that we are really worshipping and serving a created thing rather than God Himself. When we do that, we are taking a thing that is good in itself and turning it into an evil, for we are making it an idol.

Whenever we make the second choice—when we love some creaturely good more than we love God—we necessarily plunge ourselves into a downward spiral. We first choose the idol because it promises to satisfy some apparent need. What we discover, however, is that the idol does not deliver the promised satisfaction. It brings no joy or peace or contentment into our lives. But it does continue to lie to us. It tells us that we need more, and then more still. Piece by piece, we sell ourselves to the idol until eventually it takes over our lives. It comes to dominate everything, until eventually we make every decision with reference to the idol. Our own personhood is disintegrated and replaced with the desire for the idol. This spiral is a kind of long, slow descent into hell.

Just as the Holy Spirit is the earnest of our inheritance, and therefore a foretaste of heaven, the idol is an image of condemnation, and therefore a foretaste of hell. The grace that the Holy Spirit produces in us is part and parcel with the blessedness of the elect in glory. The misery that the idol produces in us is part and parcel with the sufferings of the damned who are consigned to perdition. The longer we cling to the idol, the more we come to experience what hell will be for those who are cast out of God's presence. How could it be otherwise? To pursue the idol is to hide ourselves from God's face and God's blessing.

Idols always fail to deliver what they promise. More than that, they take everything that we have. Just as the Lord our

God is a jealous God, idols are also jealous gods. They will not release their grip until they devour us. They will rob us and torture us as long as we give them any place in our lives. And as miserable as they make us, we come to feel more and more that we cannot live without them.

The longer we remain in the clutches of an idol, the stronger its hold becomes. We start to believe that we can never be happy without it (though the truth is that it brings us only misery). Because we define our lives by it, it becomes part of our identity. We feel somehow that to give up the idol would be giving up some aspect of our own selfhood. It is very much like dying.

But this dying is exactly what God calls us to do. This is the sense in which Scripture tells us that we are to kill ourselves, or rather, our earthly attachments. "Mortify therefore your members which are upon the earth; fornication, uncleanness, inordinate affection, evil concupiscence, and covetousness, which is idolatry" (Col 3:5). We are not to wait for such things to change by themselves. They never will. There is no point in negotiating with them. They seem to promise us that they will accept some compromise, but they soon strengthen their death grip once again. Difficult as it may seem, we must kill them outright.

This is a decision that is made in a moment of time. Making the decision does not mean that we will stop feeling the pull of our temptations. Indeed, the pull may feel stronger than before. The meaning of the decision is that we will stop listening to the temptation, whether our feelings change or not. Choosing a radical break with our idolatry, we must restore God to the throne of our hearts. We must acknowledge His right to bless or to withhold blessing. We must allow His will to hold sway in our lives, even if that seems to mean that we must surrender the things we hold most precious.

There is no easy way to do this, but it must be done. Otherwise, we continue the descent into hell—for ultimately, the idol takes not only all that we have, but robs us of our very identity. In the end, we become whatever our idols are. We must make the break.

Again, there is no easy way to do this. Casting down an idol is an act of faith. It is a statement that we are entrusting ourselves to God, believing that He knows what is best for us, wants what is best for us, and can do what is best for us. In a moment of decision we reject the idol and cast ourselves upon God in trust. That is repentance.

My friend, the time for repentance is now. The idol has had you long enough. Don't you realize what it has already begun to take from you? Don't you feel in your heart how it has already begun to change you into a different person—one whom you would not have recognized a few years ago? Haven't you begun to experience the torment of regret and loss and failure? Doesn't the longing for the idol grow stronger, even as its power to satisfy wanes? That is the way of idols! As the spiral continues—as you descend into hell—the pain and disintegration and loss will grow, but your strength to cast off the idol will diminish. You must repent now—you will never find a better or easier time.

Cast down the idol. Cut off every occasion for the temptation. Quit toying with this sin, utterly and completely. Stop whatever evil you are still considering. Labor to restore what you have broken. Trust God for the rest.

What is taking place in your life is not simply a conflict among your desires. It is a battle for your soul. In this world are real spiritual forces that, at the least, wish to render you useless to God and to rob you of eternal reward. These forces are doing their best to blind you to the blessings that God might intend for your life. They will whisper that you cannot go back, that the damage is too severe, that God's people (or God Himself!) will condemn you. Most of all, they will insist that your happiness can only be found in the idol. Lies! Lies!

God is living and powerful. He is merciful and good. He still wants the best for you, and He is entirely capable of changing both you and your circumstances. The real issue is simply whether you will choose to trust Him. I beg you to do just that.

IN TIME OF TEMPTATION: HIS SUFFICIENCY

Kevin T. Bauder

How came I here? A thousand times
I purposed that I would not tread
This wayward road—a thousand times
Turned I my feet in shame and dread,
Bethought me of Thy gracious smile
And cast me on Thy healing skill.
And yet, for each retreating mile,
A dozen, not against my will,
But hardly halting, onward drawn
Strode I, and further down and down,
Until my steps were well nigh gone.
What merit I, if not Thy frown?
For fear of that, I faithless fled,
And sought the darkness, where Thy face,
Now hid, might no more strike with dread.
Yet from Thee hid, I find no trace
Of peace or joy or gentleness.
Untrusting, trembling, terrified,
I cannot know Thy faithfulness.
If from the sun one turns to hide,
One cannot know the joy of light;
Thus, if I should despise Thy grace,
I must abide in graceless night.

My God, I tremble in this place.
The darkness mutters in my ears.
It whispers that Thy wrath is sure,
There is no help for all my fears,
My road has plunged me beyond cure.
Ashudder now, I taste despair
Arising in my throat. Why sob
Repentance into this black air?
I choke on fumes of guilt. They rob
My joy, corrode my moral sense,
Ignite the gulf that separates
My heart from Thine with flames of dense,
Slow, sluggish sloth that immolates
My trust in Thee.

                    Trust. Only trust.
Hast Thou not sworn? Will not Thine oath
Prevail? Could anyone more just
Confirm His testament? These both—
Thy vow and covenant—secure
Strong consolation, confident
Anticipation, to assure
My hope, anchor my soul, cement
My will to Thine. Arise my soul!
Before Him fear itself doth flee!
A flood of hope doth ever roll
Out from the Holy Place, where He
With His Own blood hath satisfied
The Law's unflinching, just demand.
Yes! In thy place the Lamb has died,
And lives, with cleansing in His hand.

EIGHT

The Communion of the Saints

e

FROM PAUL TO SPANKY: MUSINGS ON MEMBERSHIP

Jonathan Pratt

*I*n one of the episodes of the Little Rascals series Spanky and Alfalfa formed "The He-Man Womun Haters Club." This was a very elite organization, and members had to meet some high requirements: they had to be male and they had to have a great dislike for girls. While the enigmatic nature of "The He-Man Womun Haters Club" might not appeal to the readers of this essay, most can relate to the desire of belonging to a group. Back during your school days you may have joined the ski club, chess club, scouts, photo club, basketball team, or yearbook staff. And things have not changed much for us as adults either. We have exercise clubs, book clubs, business organizations, fantasy football leagues, support groups, and VFW chapters. And just like Spanky and Alfalfa's club, all of these organizations have membership requirements, guidelines that tell everyone who belongs and who does not.

The Bible also speaks of clubs or organizations. In the Old Testament, God's covenant people, the Hebrews, constituted a special group. The only requirement necessary for membership in this group was to be descended from Abraham, Isaac, and Israel. The twelve disciples were a specific group of Christ's followers, chosen directly by Him. That same group (minus Judas Iscariot) sought to identify requirements that would be used to add an apostle to their number (Acts 1:15-26). Consequently, no one should have been surprised that the organization headed by Christ and designated as His body, the church, should have specific requirements for membership. These requirements were two in number: saving faith in Jesus Christ alone and water baptism (Acts 2:41).

From Pentecost to the present day, the true church has held these requirements as necessary for identification with a local assembly. Nevertheless, in recent years two types of believers have begun to question the need for local church membership. One group consists of "universal church only" proponents who argue, "I am a member of the universal church; why should I join a local assembly?" The other group is made up of "regular attenders" who enjoy the benefits of worshipping and sometimes even of serving in a local assembly without officially joining the membership.

First, I wish to address the objection that membership in the universal church is all that the Bible requires. Why do we need the local church? Four lines of biblical evidence argue strongly against the universal church only position. Admittedly, every Christian is part of the universal church by virtue of believing in Christ. Nevertheless, these evidences indicate that every believer is responsible to join a local assembly.

The first evidence involves the role of church officers. While Christ is indeed the head of His church (Col 1:18; Eph 1:22), He has chosen to have His church led by two groups of human officials: elders and deacons (Phil 1:1; 1 Tim 3:1-13). The very existence of these human leaders in the church demands personal accountability to particular leaders. When Christians declare that their allegiance lies with Christ and that they do not need the local assembly, they choose to deny several specific New Testament commands given to *all* Christians regarding their relationships with spiritual leaders: they are to obey and submit to them (Heb 13:17); they are to respect them (1 Thess 5:12-13); and they are to give them honor (1 Tim 5:17).

Not only are commands like these rendered null and void, but Paul's exhortations to Timothy and Titus (and their churches) about the choosing of elders and deacons (1 Tim 3:1-13; Titus 1:5-9) are inexplicable if Christians are only members of the invisible, universal church. Clearly, the New Testament intends elders and deacons to serve local assemblies of believers. These elders are called to care for, lead, protect, and feed the flock; the deacons specifically function as servants to the elders and the flock. Thus, all Christians must be joined to a local, visible assembly of believers where elders and deacons serve the flock.

The second line of evidence involves the decision making process of the church. The New Testament church is frequently called upon to make its own decisions. These decisions are not delegated merely to the officers of the church but rather to the entire assembly. The assembly is to receive weak Christians into its fellowship (Rom 14:1; 15:7); it is to choose those who will serve its needy members (Acts 6:3); it is to be involved in the discipline of its members (1 Cor 5:1-5, 13); it is to punish its sinning members (2 Cor 2:6); it is responsible to send representatives that will support and voice its beliefs in other local assemblies (Acts 15:3, 22). All of these actions require a decision—probably a vote—of some type by the group of people who constitute the local assembly. Again, these types of actions by local churches are impossible if one only hails from an invisible church.

The last paragraph mentioned the discipline of members, and this constitutes the third line of evidence for church membership. Church discipline is not possible if one is not part of a visible church. People cannot be excluded from organizations to which they do not belong. Paul's call to the Corinthian church to discipline the sinful man from its midst (1 Cor 5:4-5) demands that he be a member of that assembly. The fact that Paul did not discuss the situation of the woman in this case (the man's stepmother—1 Cor 5:1) probably indicates that she was not a member of the church.

Visible membership is also assumed in regard to the duties of the assembly in discipline situations. Both Christ (Matt 18:15-18) and Paul (1 Cor 5:4-5, 13) make it quite clear that disfellowshipping a church member is never the duty of an individual. It is rather the responsibility of the entire assembly, a visible body of believers.

The final evidence for local church membership is its necessity for the proper observance of the ordinances. The ordinance of water baptism was instituted by Christ (Matt 28:19) and carried out by the apostles (Acts 2:41; 1 Cor 1:13-16). In addition to the many things that baptism symbolizes, it has always served as the *initiatory rite* of entrance into the local church. It provides public testimony of one's repentance (Acts 2:38). This aspect of water baptism is entirely unnecessary for one who claims membership in the invisible body only.

The Lord's Supper is the *continuing rite* of fellowship established by Christ for the worship of the church (1 Cor 11:23). One of the purposes of the Supper is to demonstrate the unity of the body. The intermingling of the grains in the bread signifies the oneness of the local body as it is broken into individual parts and disseminated to each one (1 Cor 10:16-17). Those who claim membership in the universal body alone miss out on the blessing of the continuing rite of the Lord's Supper and particularly of the unity that the Supper symbolizes in each local church where it is celebrated.

The foregoing has been my response to those who insist that membership in the church universal makes membership in a local church unnecessary. Now, what about those whom I have called "regular attenders?" If one can gain all the benefits that a church offers by mere attendance in the services, then why bother with membership?

Up to about fifty years ago, the vast majority of true Christians were members of the church in their locale. The idea that people would call themselves Christian but not be joined together with fellow Christians in a local church was inconceivable. How things have changed! For example, one Baptist church in the Twin Cities averages 3600 attenders but has only 1700 members. This is not an isolated phenomenon. More and more Christians are finding it easy to go to church but difficult to join.

These "regular attenders" appreciate the opportunity to join together with fellow believers in worship, and sometimes they even participate in ministry. Yet for various reasons they choose to avoid membership. I believe that such "regular attenders" are making a significant mistake. Their failure to identify in membership with their church is harmful to their individual walks with Christ and to the rest of the assembly as a whole. I can think of at least three reasons why "regular attenders" ought to join the membership of their local church.

The first reason is for accountability. When Paul spoke to the Ephesian elders in Acts 20:28, he demanded that they pay primary attention to their "flock over the which the Holy Ghost hath made you overseers." How did the elders know who was in their flock and who was not? Only those who had made a covenant commitment to the congregation could truly qualify. While elders seek to comfort, teach, and help non-members, their primary responsibility is to the members of the flock, to those who have entered into a covenant agreement with them. We do not know exactly what mechanism the apostolic churches used to indicate this covenant relationship, but some way must have existed for the elders to know which sheep were committed to their flock. In our setting and for hundreds of years, the best means we have to make this determination is church membership. Membership is a covenant relationship that allows the elders to know who is willing to receive care, warning, comfort, and instruction. Without the acknowledgement (covenant) that church membership provides, the care that the elders can give is greatly diminished.

God uses church discipline as a warning to Christians and thus as a means of sanctification.[11] When fellow members see the results of unrepentant sin, they are far more likely to take personal account of their own spiritual lives. Those who are not church members, however, are insulated from the possibility of discipline. Consequently, they deny themselves the very element of fear that would help their sanctification (2 Cor 7:8-11; 1 Tim 5:20). Certainly, being disfellowshipped from the assembly is the most extreme form of accountability, but it is a necessary and motivating one that non-members cannot appreciate.

The second reason to prefer church membership to mere attendance is to show consideration of others. How should the people in a local assembly relate to the "regular attenders?" Are they believers? Do they want to be part of the church? Should they be allowed a voice in the decisions made by the gathered assembly? Should they be permitted to minister in the nursery or choir or youth group? These kinds of tensions enter the minds of members in regard to non-members. Consequently, consideration of other brothers and sisters is a major reason for declaring one's desire for membership in a local church.

---

[11]For an extreme example, notice the effect on the church after Ananias and Sapphira were killed: "great fear came upon all the church" (Acts 5:5, 11).

Previously, I spoke of the covenant relationship between the elders and the flock that is part of church membership. The same covenant relationship applies between the members. We are all required to be devoted to one another, to honor, admonish, greet, edify, and submit to one another.[12] The only way we can know if non-members are Christians who want us to relate to them in these ways (all of which are commanded in Scripture) is for attenders to declare that they wish to enter into covenant with other Christians. Again, the mechanism we use to provide for this kind of agreement is church membership.

Even more basic issues are related to the commitments of membership. In declaring one's desire to join with a local assembly, a person is telling fellow Christians that one is a believer who agrees with the doctrinal position of the church. After someone makes this kind of declaration, all those in the assembly can have confidence that they are praying with a believer when they pray with a new member, that they are on the same theological page when they serve in ministry together, and that they can trust the new member to teach what the church's doctrinal statement affirms. But if a "regular attender" does not show consideration to his fellow Christians by officially joining the church, then the members of the church often have lingering doubts as to that attender's faith commitment.

The third reason that church membership is better than regular attendance is because it fosters obedience. Just as parents are called upon to train and discipline their children (Eph 6:4; Col 3:21), so Christians are called upon to carry out discipline in the local assembly (1 Cor 5:1-5, 13; 2 Cor 2:6). Obedience to these church discipline passages is not possible apart from membership in a local assembly.

---

[12]See Rom 12:10; 15:14; 16:16; Eph 4:12; 5:21.

Also, Christians are called upon to use their particular gifts and talents in service to the other members in the body of Christ (1 Cor 12:7, 27-31; Rom 12:4-8). Failure to serve one's fellow believers is a sin. Since church membership is the only mechanism we have to determine whether or not one is a Christian who holds to the doctrinal beliefs of our assembly, one must join the church before having the opportunity to use one's gifts in service to the rest of the body.

Church membership implies both privileges and duties. We are called to submit to our spiritual leaders, to make decisions about our church, to hold one another accountable, to show consideration to one another, and to be obedient to the commands of Scripture. Without membership in a visible local assembly it is impossible for the Christian to fulfill these God-ordained responsibilities. The requirements for church membership should include a personal testimony of salvation by faith in the gospel, baptism by immersion following salvation, agreement with the church's covenant, and a desire to glorify God with one's life. "Regular attenders" who want to worship and to serve most profitably ought to join a local church. Their spiritual life will be enhanced as they are privileged to fulfill God's commands to His people, and the church's ministry will be enhanced as God's people join forces in the cause of the gospel.

THE UNBAPTIZED BELIEVER: A BIBLICAL OXYMORON

Jonathan Pratt

*H*ow do you know that someone is a hockey player? He plays hockey. How do you know that someone is a stamp collector? She collects stamps. How do you know that someone is an auto mechanic? He fixes cars. While it is quite apparent that any three year old could answer these questions, why does the answer become so difficult when we ask, "How do you know that someone is a believer in Jesus?" The Bible is actually quite consistent in its answer to this question: he or she has been baptized.

Note, however, that I am not saying the Bible teaches baptismal regeneration. The Bible never states that the *means* by which someone becomes a believer is baptism. Quite the contrary. The Bible clearly states that the means by which someone becomes a believer is *faith* (Rom 3:28; 4:5; Gal 2:16; Eph 2:8-9). Nevertheless, the Bible affirms that baptism is the public testimony, the external demonstration, of the inner reality of faith. This is why the first believers at Pentecost were baptized (Acts 2:41). The same thing is true for the Samaritans (Acts 8:12), the Ethiopian eunuch (Acts 8:38), Saul (Acts 9:18), Cornelius (Acts 10:48), the Philippian jailer and his family (Acts 16:33), and many others. In all of these cases, people were baptized *after* they believed in order to publicly proclaim their faith. We should also notice that this external act of faith was so important that every believer in the New Testament was baptized. In fact, it is quite evident that there were no un-baptized believers in the entire New Testament after the birth of the church. Thus, if someone wanted others to know that he or she was a Christian, baptism was the means.

Baptism was significant to the believers in the NT church. It was so important that we continue the practice today. The reason we carry on the practice of baptism is the command of our Savior. Jesus expressly demanded that believers be baptized (Matt 28:19). This is why we refer to baptism as an ordinance. It is a command from Christ for the church. If Christ commanded us to be baptized, then we certainly need to be sure that we have an accurate understanding of its meaning, subjects, and mode.

The meaning of baptism carries both historical and theological significance. Historically, baptism provided the individual with a way to identify with a leader or a movement. Gentiles who desired to join the Jewish religion would submit to proselyte baptism. Similarly, when John the Baptist called upon people to repent of their sins, they showed their willingness to do so by submitting to baptism (Matt 3:11; Mark 1:5). Thus, the early church enjoyed a cultural awareness of baptism as the means of identifying with Christianity, and this traditional meaning of baptism is retained today. Almost every historically Christian denomination requires baptism for membership (though the strict requirement has been dropped in some more recent groups such as the Evangelical Free Church).

Furthermore, baptism has a theological meaning, and this prompts the question, "What exactly does baptism symbolize or illustrate?" When someone is baptized, he is providing a picture, a "word in water," of several important theological truths. First, baptism illustrates the believer's union with Christ in His death, burial, and resurrection (Rom 6:3-4; Col 2:12). Second, some believe that baptism may picture the washing and purification from sin that occurs in regeneration (Titus 3:5; Acts 22:16). Third, baptism symbolizes the truth that believers have passed safely through the waters of judgment by virtue of their union with Christ in His death and resurrection (1 Pet 3:21). Fourth, because of the similar terminology used to describe water baptism and Spirit baptism (in the former "baptism" is used literally, whereas in the latter it is used figuratively), it would appear that water baptism may symbolize Spirit baptism, which is the placing of the believer into the body of Christ (1 Cor 12:13).

What a cause of great rejoicing! The baptismal service provides a wonderful opportunity for the local church, for it is here that we observe the public proclamation of an individual's faith in Christ. This is the place where one publicly identifies with the local assembly; this is the place where we are reminded of the Christian's union with Christ in His death, burial, and resurrection; here we are reminded that we have been delivered from judgment, have had our sins washed away, and have been placed into the body of Christ.

Baptism possesses significant meaning both historically and theologically, and this meaning suggests two important implications. First, as the outward expression of the inward change wrought by the Holy Spirit, baptism is the first public act of obedience expected of the Christian. It precedes partaking of the Lord's Supper, ministry to fellow Christians in the assembly, witness of the gospel to lost sinners, and all other acts of obedience. Second, since regeneration is a work accomplished once for all, the baptism which symbolizes it (regeneration) is not to be repeated. It follows that if one has been scripturally baptized as a believer, he or she should not be baptized again.

The proper subjects of baptism can only be those who have been regenerated by the Holy Spirit. The New Testament provides clear instruction on this matter. First, the command and example of Christ and the apostles show that only disciples who have repented and believed can be baptized (Matt 28:19; Acts 2:38, 41; 8:12; 18:8). Thus, baptism always follows the exercise of saving faith. Second, the symbolism of the ordinance requires believer's baptism. Since baptism pictures one's union with Christ in His death, burial and resurrection, and since baptism proclaims one's desire to follow Christ, only one who understands and acknowledges that the saving work of Christ has been personally applied ought to be baptized. Infants are incapable of giving testimony about their belief in Christ; yet this is precisely what one does when one submits to water baptism.

The household baptism texts (e.g., Cornelius in Acts 10:2, 48, the Philippian jailer in Acts 16:29-34, and Stephanas in 1 Cor 1:16) are used by some to contradict the teaching of believer's baptism. Yet none of these texts makes reference to infants. Also, each instance speaks of belief preceding baptism (Acts 11:17; 16:34; 1 Cor 16:15). Therefore, these texts do not support infant baptism at all.

Two additional inferences follow from believer's baptism. First, since only believers who have been regenerated can be baptized, baptism itself is not the means of regeneration. Second, the church should expect credible evidence of regeneration prior to baptism (this is especially significant for children who have grown up in the church).

The mode of baptism is determined both by the meaning of the word and by the significance of the ordinance. Does the word *baptize* mean to sprinkle, to pour, or to immerse? There is surprisingly little difference over the answer to this question. The very meaning of the verb *baptizein* in Greek is "to plunge, dip, immerse" something in liquid. Every Greek lexicon lists this meaning regardless of the denominational persuasion of its authors. It is notable that the Greek Orthodox Church continues today to baptize its members by immersion. They know what the Greek word means!

The New Testament examples of baptizing indicate that immersion was the mode practiced by John the Baptist, Christ and His disciples, and the early church. In Mark 1:5 John baptized people "*in* the river Jordan" (not near or by). Jesus came up "*out of* the water" (Mark 1:10) after he was baptized. John required "much water" for baptizing (John 3:23). When Philip evangelized the Ethiopian eunuch, they stopped near the road to baptize the eunuch when "they came unto a certain water" (Acts 8:36); there would have been no need to stop at a water source if only sprinkling were required (undoubtedly the eunuch had drinking water with him). After stopping, Philip and the eunuch "went down both *into* the water" and they "came up *out of* the water" after the baptism (Acts 8:38-39).

Furthermore, the symbolism behind baptism also demands immersion. Romans 6:3-4a states: "Know ye not, that so many of us as were baptized into Jesus Christ were baptized into his death? Therefore we are buried with him by baptism into death." Burial with Christ and rising with Christ cannot be pictured by sprinkling or pouring. The union of the believer with Christ is symbolized in water baptism, and only immersion aptly demonstrates this spiritual truth.

What if someone were baptized by sprinkling or pouring after being converted? Does it really matter what the mode was if belief preceded the baptism? While we can rightly say that this is an example of a *believer* receiving pouring or sprinkling, we cannot agree that this was a scriptural *baptism* since immersion did not take place. Part of the problem in this whole discussion about mode is the translation of *baptizō*. Beginning with the early English translations, translators opted to transliterate this Greek term (i.e., "baptize") rather than giving it the proper English equivalent (i.e., "immerse"). For this reason, confusion about the mode of baptism continues to the present day. The mode, however, does matter: sprinkling is not immersing or plunging, nor is pouring. This is why any mode other than immersing cannot be considered to be scriptural baptism.

Since baptism follows faith and is not the means of faith, it is not necessary for salvation. Many great Christians (e.g., Jonathan Edwards and John Calvin) who were sprinkled as infants will be in heaven. Yet this should not keep us from seeking to be obedient to the Bible's demands concerning believer's baptism.

I appeal to my fellow brothers and sisters in Christ: if you have not yet submitted to baptism, why wait? If you are truly a Christian, you will want to proclaim this truth to everyone. In fact, if you will not be obedient to the clear teaching of the Bible, how will any of us know that you are a Christian? Athletes compete, collectors gather, mechanics fix, and Christians submit to baptism.

THE LORD'S SUPPER: CONTINUING RITE OF THE CHURCH

Jonathan Pratt

*A*dmittance into most health clubs typically involves two steps. First is the one-time initiation process. At this point applicants need to pay an entrance fee, fill out paperwork, and perhaps have a picture emblazoned on a membership card. Second is the ongoing need to show that membership card every time one seeks to gain entrance into the facility.

To a certain degree, the ordinances of the church function in this same way. Baptism is the one-time initiatory rite by which one gains acceptance into the membership of the local church. The Lord's Supper is the continuing rite that the members of the church practice regularly. The exercise of both of these ordinances flows from the commands of Christ Himself. He commanded that all believers be baptized (Matt 28:19) and that all believers observe the Lord's Supper (Luke 22:19). But what is the Lord's Supper, and what does it mean? As might be suspected, there is no uniform agreement regarding the meaning of the Lord's Supper among professing Christian churches. Four perspectives have come to be supported by various groups.

The Roman Catholic view maintains that the bread and wine of the Supper actually undergo a material change. By virtue of the consecration of the administering priest, they are turned into the actual flesh and blood of Christ. This doctrine is referred to as transubstantiation. In Catholic thought, the Lord's Supper (called the *Mass*) is viewed as a real sacrifice offered again by Christ in behalf of the worshippers. It is seen as a propitiatory offering.

It can only be administered by a properly ordained priest who must officiate at the service in order for the real transformation to take place (this idea is referred to as *sacerdotalism*).

The Lutheran view rejects the idea that the bread and wine actually become the material body of Christ, but it holds that the body and blood of Christ are present "in, with, and under" the bread and wine. An example sometimes given is that of water in a sponge. The water is not the sponge but is present "in, with, and under" the sponge and is present wherever the sponge is present. Thus, the body and blood of Christ are not the bread and wine but are present whenever these elements are present at the Lord's Table.

The Calvinistic view holds that Christ is present in the bread and wine, not physically or bodily, but spiritually. Just as the sun remains in the sky while providing warmth and light to those on the earth, so also Christ is present in the elements in this influential sense. Calvin maintained that the idea of actually eating Christ's body and drinking His blood was absurd. Rather, true believers are spiritually nourished by partaking of the bread and wine. In this view, there is a genuine, objective benefit received by the communicant. By taking the elements, communicants actually receive something of the vitality of Christ, depending upon their own faith and receptivity during the experience.

The Zwinglian view, named after its proponent, Ulrich Zwingli, sees the Lord's Supper as a commemoration. The Supper brings to mind the death of Christ and its efficacy for believers. There is no need for advocating a special presence of Christ since He is spiritually present everywhere (Matt 28:20; John 14:23). The value of the ordinance consists in remembering the benefits of Christ's death. Like a sermon, it is a type of proclamation. Unlike the sermon, the proclamation involves visible means.

In both cases, faith is essential if the participant is to gain any benefit.

To argue for the physical presence of Christ as the first two views do fails to recognize the symbolic character of Jesus' statements when He declared, "This is my body" and "This is my blood" (Mark 14:22-24). Jesus often spoke in figurative ways (e.g., John 15:1, "I am the vine," or John 10:9, "I am the door"). Especially when Jesus was eating with His disciples, they could see that He was not saying that the loaf of bread in His hand was actually His physical body. His body was seated there in front of them.

Since the body of Christ is not present in the elements, no need (or ability) exists for a human priest to transform the elements of the Lord's Supper into Christ's actual body. Certainly Jesus never suggested or practiced this Himself. He fully intended His hearers to understand that He was speaking figuratively, suggesting that the bread represented His body and that the cup represented His blood.

Additionally, the failure to recognize the clear NT statements about the once-for-all nature of Christ's atoning sacrifice (Heb 10:14) indicates a horrendous misunderstanding of Scripture. The Supper does not provide another sacrifice of Christ for sins. Jesus accomplished all that was necessary in this regard, as His words on the cross indicate: "It is finished" (John 19:30).

Christ promised that His presence would be with His followers everywhere and always (Matt 28:20; John 14:23; 15:4-7). Because of this promise, no warrant exists for some special reception of the spiritual Christ in the Lord's Supper. He also promised to be with His people when they gather together (Matt 18:20). Paul says nothing about a spiritual presence of Christ in the elements when he discusses the significance of the bread and wine in 1 Corinthians 11:26. He merely says that these elements "shew the Lord's death till he come."

Therefore, in light of these observations it would appear that the Lord's Supper is commemorative (as the Zwinglian view suggests). Christians who partake of these elements certainly do receive a blessing. They are reminded of Christ's sacrifice. They are drawn close to Him. They can come to know and love Him better through the experience. The Supper, however, does not provide some subjective encounter with the spiritual Christ. It does not transmit some type of spiritual seal by which people are assured greater eternal blessings in the future. Rather, Christians commemorate and illustrate Jesus' death as they partake.

ACTIONS AND MEANING

Jonathan Pratt

*T*he world-renowned botanist George Washington Carver was busy at work in his laboratory one day when some uninvited visitors walked in. They proceeded to traipse around the room, looking closely at all the experiments, and making a general assessment of the overall quality of his work. This was all done without receiving any permission or even acknowledging the noted professor. Finally, after the self-guided tour was completed, one of the individuals in the group went up to Carver and asked him if he would give an explanation of the experiment he was currently working on. Carver replied, "I'm sorry, your actions are speaking so loudly that I cannot hear what you are saying," and he returned to his labors without honoring the request. Actions convey meaning.

Jesus specified certain actions that ought to characterize church saints. One of these (baptism) is the initial action of a Christian by which one demonstrates personal faith in Jesus (Matt 28:19). The other action Jesus required of His followers was to observe the Lord's Supper (Luke 22:19). He intended this supper to be the continuing rite of the church ("this do…till he come," 1 Cor 11:24-26). But these ordinances of the church are not merely a demonstration of obedience to Christ's commands. They also convey meaning.

What meaning is that? What are we saying when we participate in the Lord's Supper? Furthermore, how should this meaning influence our practice at the Lord's Table?

First, as Wayne Grudem notes, "the meaning of the Lord's Supper is complex, rich, and full."[13] The Bible reveals at least six concepts that are symbolized in the partaking of this ordinance. First, the act itself symbolizes obedience to the commands of Christ ("this do," Luke 22:19) and Paul ("this do...till he come," 1 Cor 11:24-26). Second, the Lord's Supper pictures the death of Christ who gave His body (the bread) and shed His blood (the cup) on the cross for our sins. We recognize this truth in Paul's words: "ye do shew the Lord's death" (1 Cor 11:26).

Third, the symbolism of Christ's death is intended to remind the participants of that death: "this do in remembrance of me" (twice in 1 Cor 11:24-25). Thus, this symbol is a physical memorial confirming to the believer what he already affirms in his mind and heart, "Jesus died for me." This idea of remembrance by means of ceremony was frequently employed by God in the Old Testament, where Israel was enjoined to remember God's previous acts of kindness for them (e.g., Feast of Passover, Feast of Tabernacles, Feast of Dedication).

A fourth concept conveyed by the Supper is the unity of the believers who participate. This idea is seen in Paul's words in 1 Cor 10:17: "For we being many are one bread, and one body: for we are all partakers of that one bread." The elements of the communion service demonstrate a fifth truth: participation in the benefits of Christ's death (1 Cor 10:16). As we individually reach out and take the bread and the cup for ourselves, our action proclaims that we want to take the benefits of Christ's death for ourselves. When we do this, we are demonstrating symbolically that we do participate in the whole host of blessings provided by Christ in His death for His children.

Finally, the Lord's Supper helps the participants to anticipate the Lord's return. While this ceremony looks back to the death

[13]Wayne Grudem, *Systematic Theology* (Grand Rapids: Zondervan, 1994), 989.

of Christ, Christians are also looking ahead. Paul commanded his hearers to practice this ceremony "till he [Christ] come" (1 Cor 11:26). In other words, our obedience to Christ's command is only to be temporary—until He returns. Therefore, there is an implicit reminder built into the Lord's Supper itself: Christ is going to return.

When we see what is symbolized and taught by the partaking of the Lord's Supper, we begin to realize some of the richness and complexity of this important ordinance. Indeed, our actions in this ceremony convey so many different aspects of meaning that we dare not enter into it flippantly, ignorantly, or disobediently. Positively, we are blessed to show our obedience to Christ, to picture and remember His death, to demonstrate our unity in the one body, to participate in the benefits of Christ's death, and to anticipate the Lord's soon return. What a cause for thanksgiving and joy as we regularly come together to celebrate our Savior's death for us!

The various aspects of meaning should affect how we observe the Lord's Supper. Three questions come to mind in relation to the practice of the Supper. Who should participate in it? Who should administer it? How often should we celebrate it? The first of these is the most important.

Most evangelical Christians agree that only believers in Christ should celebrate the Lord's Supper. It is the continuing rite of obedience for those who are already believers in Christ. By taking the bread and cup, the participants show that they want to receive the benefits of Christ's death. Only a true believer would make such a claim.

Another important qualification of participants is that they be scripturally baptized. Those who participate in the Lord's Supper are proclaiming that they want to continue the Christian life. Why then would such people not obey Christ's initial command to proclaim that they have begun the Christian walk of faith? Baptism is the initial proclamation.

Since baptism is the only biblical way to make a public profession of personal faith in Christ, a local, visible church can only be composed of baptized believers. The Lord's Supper pictures participation in the one body, but it cannot illustrate what has not yet been established—namely, personal faith in Christ as demonstrated by water baptism. Similarly, the Lord's Table cannot symbolize unity with others in the body unless the initial act of baptism has identified one as being in the body in the first place.

Placing baptism as a prerequisite for the Lord's Table is also related to the believer's obedience. Only one ordinance is given to believers as a one-time action, and that is the command to be baptized. Since it is the public profession of faith in Christ, baptism ought to precede any other acts of obedience. To profess Christ as personal savior and yet at the same time to consciously choose to reject Christ's command to be baptized is evidence of disobedience and (possibly) unbelief.

This discussion about obedience leads to a third qualification for participants, namely, self-examination. Paul specifies who should partake of the elements: those who have examined themselves (1 Cor 11:28). The reason they should examine themselves is given in 1 Corinthians 11:27, which states that some were participating in an unworthy manner. Paul explains this unworthy manner in 11:29 as a failure in "discerning the Lord's body." Discerning the body may mean "understanding the unity and interdependence of people in the church."[14] If so, then this phrase speaks to the necessity of self-examination in regard to one's relationships in the body of Christ. Are these relationships reflecting the

---

[14]Grudem, 997.

character of the Lord? Is the communicant acting in ways that vividly portray the unity of this body?

Some in Corinth failed to undertake this kind of self-examination. As a result, they were falling under God's judgment. Some of these were becoming physically ill and some were even dying (1 Cor 11:30). It is quite obvious that God views the partaking of the Lord's Supper very seriously, especially as it relates to the unity and function of the body. Evidently, one must join together with the other members of the church in one's locale. This is one of the most significant ways of vividly portraying the unity of the body, and this suggests that one who chooses not to join his local church is actually failing to discern the body.

A final note about participants: some may have heard the terms "open," "close," and "closed" as ways of describing a church's practice of communion. In an "open" format, anyone who is saved, regardless of baptism, is invited to participate; "close" communion refers to the idea that only those who are saved and baptized can partake; a "closed" format means that only members of the local church where the Supper is being observed can participate. Most Baptist churches observe "close" communion, allowing participation by visiting believers who have been baptized but who may not be members of their church.

Who may administer the Lord's Supper? Since the Scripture gives no explicit teaching, it would be unwise to make a dogmatic assertion at this point. In light of the fact that elders have been chosen by the church to lead the church's worship, it follows that one of the elders would ordinarily officiate at the communion service. As far as distribution of the elements is concerned, it is logical that one of the deacons' duties would include this ministry. Scripture offers no reason, however, why anyone in the body could not participate in serving if asked to do so.

How often should the Lord's Table be observed? Again, Scripture provides no directive other than to observe the Lord's Supper with obedience ("as often as ye eat this bread. . ." 1 Cor 11:26). Paul seems to be saying, "I'm not telling you how often to have this ceremony, but I am telling you to have it and to observe obediently." Having the Lord's Supper every Sunday may seem to be a bit too frequent, particularly for those who have been saved out of a liturgical background where the communion service was observed ritualistically and perhaps errantly. On the other hand, celebrating the Supper only once a year, as is the practice in some Baptist churches, certainly seems to be too infrequent. Perhaps Paul's words on a different subject apply well in this case: "Let every [church] be fully persuaded in [its] own mind" (Rom 14:5).

The Lord has provided His church with a rich and valuable continuing rite. It has great value for us because of all the meaning it provides. Our actions do communicate meaning. May our churches and their members seek to relish this meaning and meditate upon these great truths each time they observe the Lord's Supper.

THE LORD'S TABLE

Kevin T. Bauder

We Baptists are often accused of taking a low view of the Lord's Supper. Sometimes that accusation almost seems fair. Occasionally some of us treat the Supper like an unimportant addendum to other services of the church. We relegate it to a place of secondary importance, prepare poorly for it, rush through it, and profit little by it. That kind of neglect, however, does not grow naturally from our view of the Lord's Table. Quite the contrary, when we understand correctly what is going on in the communion service, we shall find ourselves motivated to regard it far more seriously than we often do.

True, we do differ with Roman Catholics, Lutherans, and some Anglicans who believe that the material body and blood of Christ are present in the elements of the Supper. We even differ with some of our Reformed friends who insist that, though the body and blood may be absent, Christ is somehow really present in the bread and cup. These groups all speak of the Supper as a "sacrament." We do not object to the term if all that it means is "sacred observance," but what is usually meant is that some actual transfer of grace occurs during the partaking of the elements. Because we reject these two notions (the real presence of Christ in the elements and the sacramental transfer of grace), we are told that we have a "low view" of the Lord's Supper.

In fact, we hold a very high view indeed. We understand communion to be an ordinance that was instituted by the Lord Himself, practiced by the apostolic churches, and explained by the apostles in their writings. We observe the Lord's Table, not because we find it convenient or sentimentally meaningful, but because Christ has told us to do so. When we grasp its meaning, it exerts a deepening influence upon all of our worship and devotion.

The Lord's Supper is a memorial service that directs our attention to the cross. Jesus' command was, "This do in remembrance of me." By symbolizing the shed blood and broken body of our Lord, the elements become tangible reminders of the appalling price of our salvation. As we eat and drink, the agonies of the Lord Jesus are made present to our memories, reminding us forcefully that our sins sent Him to the tree.

When we comprehend this, we cannot approach the Table casually or flippantly. It is not a thing about which we can afford to be glib or cheery. Amidst the deep wellsprings of joy and peace that Christ has opened unto us, the Supper serves as a reminder of His dying sorrows. At the Table we grieve over the sins—our sins—that drove the nails into His hands and the thorns into His brow. We are reminded that not everything in the Christian life is polished and cheerful. All who are believers have had to face certain solemn truths, the most sobering of which is the awful penalty that Christ paid for our sins. The remembrance of His sufferings ought to be marked by an air of sober gratitude.

The Lord's Supper is also a fellowship service. That is why it is sometimes called *communion*. The communion service reminds us that Jesus lives, that sin and death are defeated foes, and that He will never leave us nor forsake us. Indeed, the Lord Himself is present at the Table. He promised His presence where even two or three were gathered in His name. He declares the local church to be the New Testament temple, the *naos*, the Holy of Holies. How then could He not be present with us? Baptists draw this distinction: while the body and blood of Jesus are not present in the *elements*, the Lord is present in the *service*. When we gather for the ordinance, we do so by His invitation. He Himself welcomes us. The observance marks a high point in our communion with Him. The Lord's Table offers the opportunity to enjoy in distilled form the same fellowship that ought to be the ongoing pattern of our lives. Thus, anything that would break our fellowship with Christ ought to bar us from the communion service. Not only the obvious sins, but also the hidden sin of neglecting Christ, must be confessed and made right before the Supper begins.

Fellowship with the Lord as our host at His Table also includes fellowship with His other guests, our brethren. We are told explicitly that the Lord's Table is to be observed "when ye come together in the church" (1 Cor 11:18). Thus, we do not celebrate private communion services, nor do we observe communion at camps, Bible conferences, or other Christian gatherings. The ordinance of the Lord's Supper is the business of the assembled local congregation. It is something that we do together as brethren. To love Christ is to love each other, and to reject each other is really to reject Christ. As John says, we have no right to profess love for God, whom we have not seen, if we do not display love for our brothers, whom we do see. At the Lord's Table, we enter together into a common memorial and act of worship. We ought never to be more at one than when we gather for *the* communion service.

Finally, the Lord's Supper is an ordinance of anticipation, "until He come." In the institution of the ordinance, Jesus pointed to a future day when He would again drink of the cup with His disciples. That day has not yet arrived. As sweet as the presence of Christ is to us now, it is not a visible or tangible presence.

The fellowship that we already enjoy passes understanding, but the fellowship that we anticipate surpasses even that. A day is coming when we shall see our Lord Jesus. He will catch us away to be with Him. In that day our communion with Him will enter its consummation. Our remaining sin and weakness will be left behind. All bars and blockages to His presence will be finally removed. Thus, every communion service involves the anticipation of Jesus' return and of the complete and untrammeled ravishment of our souls by Him.

This is how Baptists understand the Lord's Supper. Both sacramentalism and flippancy are out of place in the communion service. We receive no new grace by partaking of the elements, but we are led into deeper levels of reflection, gratitude, reverence, self-examination, communion, and anticipation. We are right not to make too much of the Lord's Supper. We are also right not to make too little of it.

BRETHREN, WE NEED EACH OTHER

Dan Brown

*B*aptists prize the autonomy of their local churches. They wear the doctrine of independence as the king wears his regal robe. Independence does not apply only to unaffiliated Baptist churches. Baptist churches that fellowship with associations, conferences, and conventions may accept a measure of accountability, but even they insist that they are independent.

Baptists have no pope, diocese, or synod. Baptist independence involves refusing ecclesiastical interference as well as political interference. This independence works both for and against Baptists. Filling pastoral vacancies and helping struggling churches are two areas in which independence creates difficulty. Independent Baptists do not always have the best track record when it comes to working with each other. The lack of perspective for the greater body of Christ can cause us to have such a narrow focus that all we can see is our own ministry. A narrow focus upon our own ministry can lead either to a feeling of inadequacy (an inferiority complex) or to a feeling of arrogance (a superiority complex).

One area in which Baptist brethren can and should depend upon one another is in church councils. Significant doctrinal issues have often been settled by the gathering of the greater body of Christ to respond to doctrinal deviation. Such councils have usually been called in response to deep division within the church.

Typically, these councils consist of two groups: a host church and a gathering of messengers who are invited by that host church. The host congregation invites churches of like faith and order to send pastors and brethren as messengers. These messengers meet in an advisory capacity for some purpose specified by the host church. The inviting church may, at its own discretion, invite other individuals to participate.

Baptist polity allows for at least two types of church councils. Both types exist in order to assist local churches. Both may reasonably be inferred from New Testament principles.

The first type of church council is the ordination council. In this case, a local church invites sister churches to assist in the examination of a man whom the church believes to be called to ministry. The church asks the ordination council to provide expertise in areas in which the church members themselves might not be proficient. The council questions the candidate about his salvation, call, and doctrine. The council will then offer an opinion to the church as to the advisability of proceeding with the ordination.

The ordination council performs a vital biblical function. Scripture cautions elders to use careful discernment before formally placing a man into the ministry (1 Tim 5:22). The ordination council provides the ordaining church with an opportunity to have elders from many congregations examine the man on whom they will lay hands.

The second type of church council among Baptists is the recognition council. The recognition council is called by a church that is newly being organized. Prior to its chartering service, it asks a council to examine and advise it regarding its covenant, articles of faith, and constitution.

The recognition council serves two important functions. First, it can provide expertise and advice that will help the fledgling church to prevent future problems. Changes in the church's documents, and especially the doctrinal statement, can be made easily before the church is formally organized. Following the chartering service, however, such changes generally become more difficult.

A church may prove to be irregular in doctrine or practice, or "out of order." If so, then the recognition council can and should help with errors of faith and practice. Many such errors are committed unwittingly, and fledgling churches welcome the opportunity to correct them.

The second important function served by the recognition council is that it acquaints established churches with the new congregation. Because their messengers have examined it, they know whether it is truly a church of like faith and order. This facilitates the process of fellowship with the new church, and it removes hesitation about recommending it to prospective members who move into its neighborhood.

Three closing observations about church councils are in order. First, the decisions of a church council are recommendations and nothing more. Councils do not legislate or adjudicate. Councils do not supersede the autonomy of the local church at any point. Baptists prioritize the autonomy of the local church. Therefore, receiving the recommendations of a council might be prudent, but their recommendations are not binding.

Second, church councils are temporary, usually lasting only a few hours. The *ad hoc* nature of church councils requires certain parliamentary proceedings that are often misunderstood. The council, having never previously existed, votes itself into existence so that it can operate decently and in order just long enough to accomplish its assigned business. When that business is complete, it dissolves—never to meet again.

Finally, the invitation to participate in a church council places an obligation upon the invited church and pastor. Every invited church has a fraternal responsibility to the inviting church to respond with its presence. This means attending and participating, even at the cost of time and finances. In fact, an invited pastor is obligated to attend unless providentially hindered, especially if a prior working relationship exists between the churches. The next request for a council could come from you.

God permits churches to help each other. God permits churches to advise each other. This mutual support and advice is one of the great blessings of New Testament church order. Brethren, we need each other.

NINE

Expectation

THOSE PESKY PREMILLENNIALISTS

Kevin T. Bauder

*D*isagreeing with someone's perspective is one thing, but dismissing it is something else. People can disagree respectfully. Respectful disagreement involves listening carefully to other individuals in conversations, understanding their positions, and considering carefully the arguments that favor them (or that weigh against one's own position) before replying. When a perspective is dismissed, however, it is rejected as so implausible—and perhaps so damaging—that it does not warrant a hearing. Dismissiveness is often accompanied by derision.

In certain theological circles, premillennialism, especially in its dispensationalist varieties, is almost habitually dismissed and derided. A recent example involves a sermon preached by a well-known evangelical pastor. The sermon, which was partly addressed to premillennial pastors, was mainly an exposition of Revelation 20. To be clear, the sermon contained much useful teaching. This influential pastor, however, began his treatment of the text by repeating a quip that Revelation is not "for the armchair prophets with their charts of historical events and their intricate diagrams of the end of the age." He then continued, "This is not rightly dividing the Word of Truth," a clear allusion to dispensational theology. He insisted that the purpose of the book of Revelation is to provide "warning and reassurance" to "harassed, subsistence-level Christians," to "encourage them in their struggle," and to "liberate them from fear of the enemy within and without." In other words, the purpose of Revelation is to hearten persecuted believers, not to disclose details of an eschatological timetable.

Those two activities, however, are not mutually exclusive. Granted, the purpose of the Apocalypse really is to encourage perseverance among believers who are facing oppression. Even so, that does not imply that eschatological chronology or detail is necessarily absent from the book. It is at least possible that the details of eschatological chronology might be revealed in order to provide motivation for perseverance.

At this point, a concession is in order. Even if eschatological detail and chronology are important, not every use of these details is necessarily helpful. In fact, two uses of prophetic schematizing are damaging. These uses ought to be an embarrassment to every responsible premillennialist.

One bad use of biblical prophecy is to satisfy mere curiosity about the future. Some people experience a kind of nosiness about things to come. To satisfy this desire, unscrupulous individuals have created an entire occult industry that purports to peer into the future. Some people read biblical prophecy for much the same reason that others read Nostradamus or consult their daily horoscopes. This practice surely misses the point.

A second bad use of prophecy is to turn it into a source of entertainment. Some dispensationalists have invented a literary genre that could be called "prophetic fiction." In their novels and movies, they surround biblical prophecies with action-packed story-telling and extra-biblical speculation. Treated this way, prophecy becomes fantasy. Some people read *Left Behind* for much the same reason that others read *Harry Potter*. Turning prophecy into amusement almost invariably debases it.

Such uses of prophecy are harmful, but they do not count against the suggestion that biblical prophecy reveals eschatological chronology or detail. Whether or not Scripture includes those details can only be determined by examining the Scriptures themselves. If the text actually communicates eschatological chronology and details, then chronology and details must be important and ought to be studied.

Not surprisingly, the dispute over eschatological detail soon turns into a dispute over the proper way of reading prophetic passages. Those who deride eschatological detail often assume that prophetic texts should be read in a non-literal way. On the other hand, those who read the texts in a literal way usually affirm the importance of eschatological detail.

The word *literal*, however, lends itself to misunderstanding. Premillennialists (especially dispensationalists) have sometimes contributed to this misunderstanding by failing to clarify what they mean by their use of the term. Too often, "literal" seems to be opposed to "literary," disallowing any figurative or symbolic uses of language.

Responsible premillennialists know better. They are fully prepared to grant the multiple levels at which ordinary language communicates. What they are not prepared to concede is that biblical prophecies ought to be read in a way that wholly exempts them from the ordinary use of language. Premillennialists are not prepared to concede that figurative or symbolic uses of language authorize the wholesale spiritualization of prophecy.

Premillennialists—particularly dispensationalists—note that biblical prophecy may be divided into two broad classes. Some prophecies have been wholly and indisputably fulfilled. The fulfillment of other prophecies remains wholly or partly in the future.

The prophecies that have already been fulfilled provide a convenient way of understanding how prophetic language works. By noting how these prophecies were fulfilled, interpreters can develop a hermeneutic for interpreting prophecy. The same hermeneutic may then be applied to unfulfilled prophecy.

If interpreters do engage in that exercise, then what conclusions will they draw? The answer is that they are very likely to become premillennialists. Indeed, this kind of reading is what premillennialists mean by "literal" interpretation. Incidentally, the habit of reading prophetic Scriptures in this way is one of the marks of dispensationalism.

Prophetic chronology and eschatological detail are not antithetical to spiritual encouragement. Interpreters will be able to determine whether prophetic passages include detailed chronology only by studying those passages. As they explore the prophetic texts, unfulfilled prophecies ought to be understood in the same way in which fulfilled prophecies have received their fulfillment. If prophetic passages, when interpreted in this way, actually do include eschatological details and chronological markers, then those things are part of the whole counsel of God. Whatever is in the Word of God is worthy of being studied, believed, and taught.

So, what about charts? Would non-dispensationalists really be happier if dispensationalists simply refused to use charts? It seems unlikely.

All sorts of people, including theologians, use charts, diagrams, and graphic representations to help them visualize all sorts of things. Biblical geography can be represented cartographically. Greek and Hebrew professors expect their classes to do sentence diagrams. The history of Israel is often taught using charts and diagrams. The relationships of biblical characters can be charted in a family tree. John Bunyan even published a map showing the differences between the covenant of grace and the covenant of works. Charts can be very useful in distinguishing doctrines such as redemption, propitiation, and reconciliation.

Many non-dispensationalist teachers use charts for a variety of purposes. Charts can be used to help people conceptualize geographical, grammatical, historical, genealogical, and soteriological relationships. Why should they not be used to help people conceptualize eschatological ones?

Premillennialists use charts. So what? They see detail and chronology in eschatological passages. So what? They think that eschatological details matter when those details are taught by the Word of God. So what?

None of these considerations constitutes a real objection to premillennialism or even dispensationalism. None of them constitutes a legitimate, *prima facie* warrant for dismissing premillennial eschatology. A more appropriate response would be to treat premillennialism as a responsible alternative within the theological matrix, even if one must disagree with it.

Our Eternal Occupation

Kevin T. Bauder

C hristian writers from Augustine to Dante picture the eternal destiny of the righteous as beatific vision. The idea is that in eternity, purified from our sins and glorified in our resurrection bodies, we shall behold God in the fullness of His glory. Transfixed with His beauty, our eyes shall gaze upon Him in a kind of everlasting stare. We shall neither want nor need anything other than to behold His presence and to enjoy His glory.

According to this theory, the redeemed in heaven are the subjects of a more-or-less perpetual trance. The theory is elegant in its simplicity, but it leaves a certain number of loose ends. If all we are meant to do is to gaze upon eternal glory, then why do we need bodies at all? Why put God through the bother of raising us from the dead when disembodied souls would do as well? For that matter, why would we need a new earth? Wouldn't a strictly spiritual heaven suit the purpose as well or better? To go a step further, why should God ever have bothered with material creation at all if His ultimate purpose was to engage the minds of His people so completely as to render their bodies superfluous?

When we look at the opposite end of redemption history—the creation—we find that spirituality and materiality complement one another in God's plan. God creates humanity as male and female. He makes them as people who do material things such as eating and reproducing. He gives them material trees with tangible fruit for their food. He surrounds them with material objects of interest. They are able to tell seasons by looking at celestial bodies. They are given opportunity to practice taxonomy on the phyla of animal creation.

God places His people in paradise, but it is not an ethereal utopia. It is a specific land, marked out by rivers, and stretching from Cush to modern Iraq. It contains precious metal and gemstones. To be sure, the original creation included a spiritual dimension—the Lord God walked and spoke with His creatures in the Garden. Nevertheless, paradise was irrefragably material, and the presence of God was not the sole object of human attention.

In fact, part of the way that humans were intended to enjoy and glorify God meant looking *away* from Him rather than looking *at* Him. For example, when Adam named the animals, he was looking at lions and tigers and bears, not at God. By looking away from God, he actually learned more about God, for he was able to discern God's character when he saw it reflected in God's *poiema*. The naming of the animals also gave Adam the opportunity to perform a task to the glory of God. If Adam had refused to shift his gaze from the divine presence, then he would actually have missed an occasion to worship and serve God.

There is an important lesson here. We humans discover God's character by looking at what God does. His mighty works of creation and redemption are the arena within which He puts Himself on display. That is why *most* of the Bible is a story, and *all* of the rest of the Bible is reflection upon that story.

There is also another lesson. We worship God, not merely by enjoying His presence and offering Him our praises, but also by serving Him. Serving Him requires us to focus, not upon God Himself, but upon the task that we are performing for His glory. For example, a believing surgeon glorifies God best, not by holding a prayer meeting in the middle of the operating room, but by paying attention to what he is doing while he operates.

Admittedly, Adam had moments when God was the object of his full attention. There were times when Adam was permitted to look at God, and there were times when he was required to look away. Bringing glory to God required Adam to do both, to oscillate between the beatific vision and the everyday things of the world, to alternate between the sacred and the mundane—except that, when the ordinary things of this world are used to reveal God's character and as tools in our service for God, then they, too, become sacred.

Everything in Eden was sacred because everything (material and immaterial alike) was devoted to the glory of God. Everything in our lives should become sacred in exactly the same sense. For the true worshipper of Jehovah, nothing is common.

As it was in the beginning, and as it is now, so it ever shall be, world without end. God does not intend for us to sit eternally in a celestial trance. To be sure, there will be moments of pure adoration when we add our voices to the mighty choir of patriarchs, prophets, apostles, and martyrs. We, too, shall cast our crowns at His feet. We, too, shall exalt the worthiness of the Lamb.

That being said, there is still the new earth, the holy city, the river, the tree of life, the nations, and our own resurrection bodies. While none of these things will be exactly natural, they will be material. Materiality must have some purpose, even in eternity future. Why should it be unthinkable that we might be required to shift our gaze away from the divine Shekinah in order that we may see the many splendors of God's glory reflected in what He does and has done? Why should it be unreasonable to suppose that He might have some task for us to perform, some exercise of mind and limb, to which we must direct our attention in order to honor Him?

Eternity is spiritual. That is certain. But eternity is also material. These do not contradict each other.

ABOUT THE EDITOR

Dr. Kevin T. Bauder is Research Professor of Systematic Theology at Central Baptist Theological Seminary of Minneapolis. He holds a D.Min. from Trinity Evangelical Divinity School, along with a Ph.D. from Dallas Theological Seminary. He and his wife, Debra, live in Crystal, Minnesota. They have two adult children.